Newsworthy

Newsworthy

Media Relations Without the Spin

donalee Moulton

Clare O'Connor

BEP

BUSINESS EXPERT PRESS

Leader in applied, concise business books

Newsworthy: Media Relations Without the Spin

First published in 2026 by
Business Expert Press, LLC
222 East 46th Street, New York, NY 10017
www.businessexpertpress.com

ISBN-13: 978-1-63742-918-1 (paperback)
ISBN-13: 978-1-63742-919-8 (e-book)

Corporate Communications Collection

First edition: 2026

10 9 8 7 6 5 4 3 2 1

EU SAFETY REPRESENTATIVE
Mare Nostrum Group B.V.
Mauritskade 21D
1091 GC Amsterdam
The Netherlands
gpsr@mare-nostrum.co.uk

Dedication

To Amy, who has always understood there is no spotlight
without working diligently behind the scenes.
With love
donalee

For Meredith, you make it all possible.
With love and gratitude, Clare

Description

Building a strong brand and a solid reputation both require building an effective relationship with media. This book serves as a comprehensive guide for professionals aiming to enhance media relations within their organization and strengthen interview skills for spokespeople and themselves.

Newsworthy: Media Relations Without the Spin offers strategies for establishing meaningful connections with media professionals, understanding the intricacies of newsworthiness, and addressing the current challenges faced by journalists. It also offers practical tips on conducting effective interviews across television, radio, online, and print; leveraging social media for storytelling; and crafting compelling news releases, backgrounders, and pitches.

Readers will benefit from:

- *Enhanced Media Relations Skills.* Craft compelling pitches, build trust with journalists, and effectively manage media interactions, leading to more favorable media coverage and improved brand reputation.
- *Understanding Newsworthiness.* Gain a clear understanding of what makes a story newsworthy to better tailor pitches to capture media interest.
- *Navigating Modern Journalism Challenges.* This insight will help foster positive relationships and ensure messages resonate.
- *Target Audience Insights.* Craft messages that effectively reach and engage different demographic groups, enhancing the impact of all communications.
- *Interview-Success Techniques.* Learn how to effectively prepare, handle challenging questions, and present confidently.
- *Leveraging Social Media.* Discover how to amplify messages and engage with audiences through social media.
- *Crafting Effective Media Documents.* Practical guidance on writing key media documents, including news releases, backgrounders, position papers, and personality profiles.

Contents

List of Figures

Review Quotes

"*Read* Newsworthy: Media Relations Without the Spin. *It will get you earned media—and earned media is essential. It gets quoted, repeated, shared; it makes you and your organization an authority; and it is noted by other media who put you at the top of their list to contact for future stories.*"
—Allan Lynch, Reporter and Former Managing Editor and Publisher

"Newsworthy: Media Relations Without the Spin *is clear, straightforward, easy-to-understand and follow. I read it in one sitting and really enjoyed it.*"
—Cathy Jacob, Writer, Leadership Coach, and Former Communications Consultant. Author of *The Slow Sip* (a Substack newsletter)

Acknowledgments

As professional writers, we know the words you read in this book live and breathe because a team of editors, proofreaders, reviewers, and others stood in the wings with their pens and penchants for perfection at the ready. We thank you for your feedback and your thoughtfulness. In particular, we would like to extend our gratitude to Debbie DuFrene, editor of the Corporate Communications Collection at Business Expert Press for her thoroughness and her support of this work. We are also indebted to Cheryl Enman with Quantum Communications who read and reread the book. Then formatted the book. Then read it again.

As communications professionals, we know the content of this book lives and breathes because clients, students, mentors, mentees, and others have shared their experiences and insights with us. This has enabled us in the moment and over the decades to more comprehensively understand the world of media relations, its challenges and its promise. You have motivated us, informed us, and helped us to refine our thinking, our concepts, and our awareness of the world as it really is and as it could be.

Finally, as women with full, busy lives, we know the words in this book live and breathe, this content resonates and deepens because of the people in our lives who have absolutely nothing to do with media relations. These are the people who love us, who understand that when we should be relaxing—with them—we are compelled to organize, to weave words together, to write. These are the people who rejig schedules and dash out the door on errands because our meetings run late or we're on a roll and don't want to interrupt the flow.

These are our family and friends. And they are the reason this book exists.

Foreword

Not so very long ago, neighborhood children on bicycles delivered daily newspapers. Today, instead of reading about what happened the day before, we watch live video of the news of the moment, from nearly anywhere on, above, or below the surface of the earth.

1970s sci-fi come to life: Globally connected social media delivers the world into your hand, a world in which almost everyone has a camera and a microphone.

This change, this digital transformation, has been relentless, and it's not slowing but quite the opposite: it's going ever faster. The morning paper fully morphed into the 24-hour news cycle.

The relentless, incremental changes become vast and disruptive. It's easy to feel as though nothing is the same.

But that's not true. There are fundamentals in our world, despite the digital transformation of so much of our daily lives. For example, you shouldn't pick a cat up by the tail. There is no such thing as a free lunch. We make our mistakes in public. Relationships still matter.

Like the authors of this book, I've been immersed in the public relations environment for a few decades. It covers a slew of roles: crime and politics reporter for network TV, features writer for magazines, photojournalist and videographer, corporate and nonprofit board member, event producer, owner of multiple communications and digital design companies. Clients from traditional to new media, governments, corporations, national and local associations, nonprofits and individuals. All tied together by the need to understand my audiences and communicate with them or for them.

We often tend to think of public relations as two opposing teams trying to put one over on the other. Yes, that happens. But for the most part, we share more than we differ: Our goal is to communicate clearly and effectively to our audiences, often targeting the very same audience.

Despite all the hype and partially successful introduction of off-the-shelf generative artificial intelligence into our lives, humans still rule the roost. In sane organizations, humans are the gatekeepers who validate and own the end product. Our humanness can be mimicked, yet remains unique to us.

This is where relationships—with the people on both sides, with the truth, with the interconnectedness of seemingly disparate forces, with the human inside us—are critical.

The book you're holding in your hand will take you on a journey through a changing landscape, while providing you landmarks and understandings so you can chart your own path.

Cheers,

George Butters

CEO, Smartypants.com Inc.

CHAPTER 1

Inside Media Relations

"Earned media is the most trusted and credible form of content for a brand or organization."

—*Ad Age* magazine

So, What Is Earned Media?

Quite simply earned media is what media relations is all about. It's coverage you don't pay for. Coverage you have earned for a variety of reasons. Perhaps you have developed a reputation as being a solid source of knowledge, a voice with impact, or an organization with an innovative way of seeing the world.

Either way, earned media is the opposite of advertising, which means less impact on your budget. Despite this being a distinct advantage, it's not the biggest.

The fact that you have been organically mentioned gives your organization the ever-important stamp of credibility.

While paid advertising is rightly seen as a one-way message delivered with a vested self-interest, earned media is generated by those outside your organization. It translates into receptivity. People are more open to hearing about what you're doing and why; they are more likely to support your organization, buy your product, endorse a policy you propose. Listeners and readers become aware—or more aware—of your organization without feeling like they are being "sold" something. They get a better understanding of your purpose, your product, and your policies without feeling that the information source is one-sided.

Earned media is also more likely to get you quoted, quoted again, and shared on social media. This is, in part, because it makes you and/or your organization an authority. That credible voice of authority is then noted by other media who may put you at the top of their contact list for future stories.

In what feels like a hyperpolarized global political environment, gaining earned media is more beneficial—and more complicated—than ever. The distinction between opinion, analysis, and hard news is getting blurry and trust in the messenger is becoming more and more dependent on individual belief systems.

However, despite the challenges, there is a path forward.

It's one that involves what can be scary to some, routine to others, and incredibly satisfying to many, including the two of us. You need to build a relationship with the media. You need to plan what that relationship will look like and how it will unfold.

That is not an easy task. Media is now defined differently, more broadly, than it once was. And there are different rules. However, the two key factors that were the hallmark of solid media relations in the past remain intact: interpretation and intention.

For many organizations in the public, private, and nonprofit sectors, a relationship with the media is defined as one that benefits them exclusively. It's seen as an opportunity to educate the media about what they do and the value of that work. An opportunity to mitigate bad or potentially harmful news. An opportunity to get their name in the news and in front of thousands, perhaps even millions, of people.

Many organizations believe media relations is intended to give them an advantage in the press, to be quoted first, to be noted in an article or in a broadcast, to get free publicity and credibility.

Admittedly, media relations can be all of those things, or more accurately deliver on all of those goals, unspoken, whispered, or otherwise. But that is not effective media relations, and you can bet that philosophy will result in a short-lived relationship.

Effective media relations recognizes that a sustained, successful relationship is symbiotic. Both parties benefit, both parties compromise, both parties set boundaries. Both parties give something, and both parties get something.

As with any relationship, finding common ground, growing together, and maintaining respect, doesn't just happen. You need to work at it. For organizations, that means formalizing their relationship internally so that those people who interact with the media do so consistently and transparently.

It means making a plan. Defining your part in the relationship and what you want and need to get out of it.

And when you have been mentioned, when you have been the beneficiary of earned media, it will be due, at least in part, to the solid media relations strategy that transcends any one individual's presence in your organization. It, in fact, is so embedded in your organizational culture that anyone can understand its direction and follow its path.

Still reticent?

That may be because you worry no one will follow the plan or because, even with an approved plan that has been endorsed by your most senior leaders, someone will still go off script. Or maybe because you don't have the time or resources.

A plan doesn't fix everything. It won't bring resources you don't have and it may not reign in the person who ad libs too often. However, a media relations plan helps manage those things—and more.

It is also a protective coating of armor against the sword of Damocles that hangs over many organizations and those who lead them. It's spelled c-r-i-s-i-s. A crisis—public outcry, natural disaster, uprising, environmental or other catastrophe—draws intensive and extended media coverage. Remember the Deepwater Horizon oil spill, commonly called the BP oil spill?

Here's a brief trip back in time.

In the spring of 2010, an explosion occurred on a drilling platform in the Gulf of Mexico that killed 11 people, sank the rig, and spewed forth 134 million gallons of oil. According to a Pew Research Center report "100 Days of Gushing Oil—Media Analysis and Quiz," the spill dominated mainstream news, accounting for 22 percent of news in the 100-day period after the explosion—almost double the next biggest story. In the 14 weeks included in the Pew study, the disaster ranked among the top three weekly stories 14 times. And it registered as the number one story in nine of those weeks.

The crisis and its very public visibility had an adverse effect on the company's reputation. In their paper "Penalties for industrial accidents: The impact of the Deepwater Horizon accident on BP's reputation and stock market returns," researchers William McGuire, Ellen Alexandra Holtmaat, and Aseem Prakash found that "in the aftermath of the Deepwater accident, BP's reputation declined by approximately 50% relative to the synthetic control [similar to a control group], and this decline persisted through the end of 2017."

From a media relations point of view, living through a crisis and the media maelstrom that inevitably follows is just the first step. The spotlight will be unrelenting, the heat scorching. Then comes the aftermath. When the crisis dies down, as all crises do, your key audiences (the public, customers, supporters, donors, and more) are left with a very specific image of your organization and how it behaved when behaving well mattered most. In the aftermath of a crisis, your organization's reputation can continue to be damaged—or it can improve. It all depends on how the crisis was handled.

Case Study

Maple Leaf Foods

On August 20, 2008, Maple Leaf Foods, a Canadian food-production company, announced a voluntary product recall. An outbreak of listeriosis was subsequently linked to one of the company's plants in Ontario. Consequently, 57 people contracted the disease, and 23 died.

The company is widely applauded for its handling of the crisis, particularly president and CEO Michael McCain. In his study "Authentic Crisis Leadership and Reputation Management: Maple Leaf Foods and 2008 Listeriosis Crisis," Dr. Terry Flynn, director of the Master of Communication Management Degree Program at McMaster University, measured more than 4,600 Canadians' perceptions of Maple Leaf Foods before, during, and after the crisis. Under the microscope: their reputational opinions, loyalty, trust, and future desire to do business with the company.

Because of the company's handling of the crisis, which included extensive media coverage and ongoing media relations, its reputation rebounded—and then some—in less than five months.

The numbers speak for themselves. Three months prior to the recall and the outbreak, data collected by Leger Marketing found 74 percent of respondents gave the company a "good" rating and 7 percent a "bad" rating. During the crisis, only 57 percent of customers rated the company "good" and 34 percent rated it "bad." In the aftermath of the crisis, these numbers were a thing of the past. "Good" ratings hit 88 percent and "bad" ratings dropped back to 7 percent.

The study also notes that those participants who saw the video news releases produced and distributed by Maple Leaf Foods had significantly higher good opinion ratings than those that didn't see the video (74 percent vs. 63 percent).

Managing a crisis, showing audiences that your organization deserves their business, attention, and/or support, is not just about avoiding a falling sword, it's about being ready when it does.

As illustrated in Figure 1.1, an intentional, formal media relations plan provides value both internally and externally.

A Formal Media Relations Plan

Recognizes
Shared
Interests

Enables
Internal
Clarity

Engenders Trust

Demonstrates
Transparency

Reinforces
Credibility

Reduces
Misinformation
Spread

Strengthens Reach

Enhances
Message
Receptivity

Figure 1.1 Value of relationships in communications

What's in It for the Media?

Eloquent as it sounds, lots. As mentioned previously, a sustained, successful relationship works for both parties. You understand how media relations can help you. You also need to understand how it can benefit the media outlet.

Reporters often have to turn stories on a dime. That is especially true in a digital age when users expect—and often demand—breaking news and updates to be available within minutes. That means journalists need to have experts, spokespeople, and other relevant contacts they can rely on to speak out or provide background, and quickly. If organizations want the media to consider their issues, stories, and ideas, they need to show the same courtesy when the media reaches out.

The media also demand professionalism. Having a healthy relationship with media outlets and specific journalists, does not mean they "owe" you anything. This is not tit for tat. This is about understanding the role each party plays in a news story, or any story, and respecting that sometimes you'll like the outcome and sometimes you won't. But both parties always have the right to say no.

Today, those parties extend beyond what was once mainstream and traditional news outlets (newspapers, TV, radio). This group now includes bloggers and influencers. In these realms, immediate access to information is even more crucial as they go to "print" in the press of a button. Instead of oversight by editors demanding at least two sources, opinion, interpretation, and bias may become suitable narrators. Then there are errors made in good faith but not fact checked.

It is important to note that there are differences between mainstream reporters and bloggers and influencers. Reporters are telling a story and will get paid even if that story doesn't run. Influencers and bloggers are making a living building a brand—and giving you access to their followers. This may come at a cost. Often there are also different motivations, even ethics at play.

In one of his blog posts, Randall Craig, CEO of the Braintrust Professional Institute, acknowledges errors, how they happen, and how to avoid and repair inaccuracies. He notes in a Facebook post, he relied on third-party sites and "quoted" Albert Einstein as saying, "Problems cannot be solved by the same level of thinking that created them." Unfortunately, Einstein never said this.

Another dynamic at play includes the ever-present "comments" section. Even when you are pleased with coverage that has provided an accurate picture and properly identifies your organization, offers well-articulated quotes, and may even make you pause for a moment of pride. But then you read on and see that the comments section is interspersed with negativity. With or without a plan, the worst thing you can do is ignore these. We're not suggesting you have to reply to every single comment, but built into your plan, there must be a method for dealing with the comment section. When working with organizations, we have suggested three key questions to ask yourself and/or your team.

Three key questions:

1. Do the comments provide items you can use as a suggestion for better improving a function of your business or service? If so, dive into this as a quality-improvement recommendation. This will enable you to also respond to the comment with a note of gratitude and "here's what we're doing about it." Responding to comments takes time, but it is important to do this without being on defense.

2. Can the comments be used to develop a dashboard within your organization or to add to an existing one regarding reputation management? If so, they may be useful at a strategic PR level. You can map them out and use them to measure whether or not your media relations plan is working. Is the negativity trending upward or down?

3. Where are the comments coming from? This is especially important if you are a larger company and have an online sales approach versus store front. Either way, if you can gain perspective on where the comments (good and bad) are coming from, it may help offer insight you would otherwise gain from focus groups, into how your services are landing with your audiences and, if possible, even demographic groups.

Using the "Comment" Section for Improvement

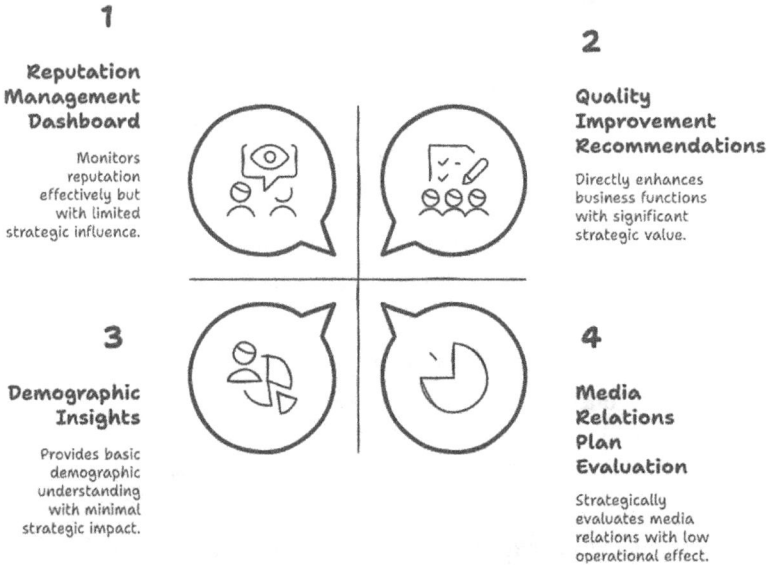

1

Reputation Management Dashboard

Monitors reputation effectively but with limited strategic influence.

2

Quality Improvement Recommendations

Directly enhances business functions with significant strategic value.

3

Demographic Insights

Provides basic demographic understanding with minimal strategic impact.

4

Media Relations Plan Evaluation

Strategically evaluates media relations with low operational effect.

Figure 1.2 Using the comment section

This is visually laid out in Figure 1.2 and then elaborated upon.

The bottom line is that the comments section should not be feared but used to provide you with important information you would not have had access to in the past. There will always be negativity. Whether or not you have a media relations plan, this is a fact. You will never gain 100 percent approval. But this is a marathon not a sprint. You might as well make use of the pit stops along the way to refuel.

What if I Don't Want to Play?

You don't have to. Nowhere is it written that organizations must think strategically about their relationship with the media. Many don't (although we would argue the more successful ones do).

Your media relations plan can be no plan at all. You can refuse interviews, decline to comment, rely on advertising and social media to build awareness and to build your brand. The media is unlikely to seek you out unless there is a crisis or controversy. Then they will run with stories, and you will be part of those stories whether you want to or not. And those stories will often note that you declined to comment, did not return messages, or offered up only a scripted e-mail response. In some cases, there may even be a limited attempt to reach you before declaring you nonresponsive, especially when you do not have a solid media relationship.

The bottom line: You will not come out of this smelling like a rose.

There are two broad approaches to media relations: proactive and reactive. Many organizations don't understand how the media works. They distrust them. The thought of reaching out to media and consorting with the enemy is anathema. These organizations keep their heads down and go about doing their work. Often, successfully so.

They are, however, missing out on important opportunities to share their stories and their expertise with their community, and perhaps the world. They are also not immune. If controversy or crisis erupts, the media will come calling. Keeping your head buried in the sand is not a recommended response. In the absence of experience working with media, however, it may be preferable to mishandling the situation while the world watches.

Numerous companies, government departments and agencies, and nonprofits look at media relations not just as an opportunity but as an essential component of doing their work. They don't react, they prepare. They develop media plans and policies. They work with media. They keep their heads above ground and focused on the issues and opportunities in front of them. The diagram in Figure 1.3 highlights the differences between the two approaches.

Where people get their news has changed, especially in the wake of digital transformation and the COVID-19 pandemic, but there is still a large and robust audience out there seeking information from credible news sources. The Pew Research Center in their Newspapers Fact Sheet— Fact Sheets: State of the News Media reported that in 2022, estimated total U.S. daily newspaper circulation (print and digital combined) was 20.9 million a day—every day of the week.

Two Broad Approaches

Proactive

Opportunities Await
Prepare and
Capitalize

Reactive

Opportunities missed
Scramble and Hope for the
Best

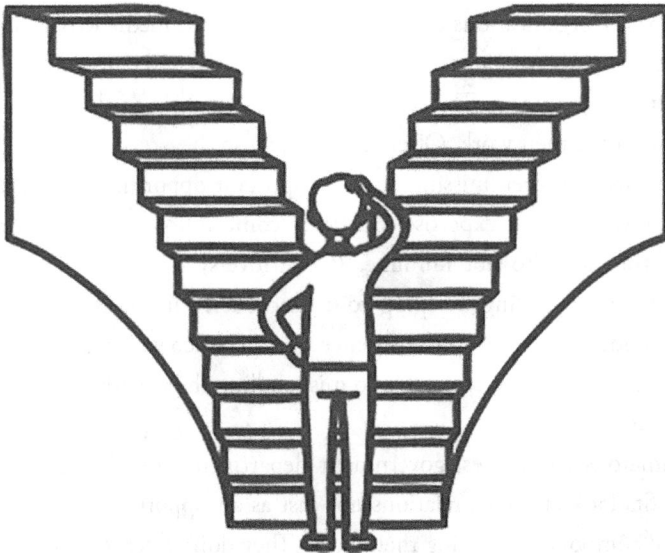

Figure 1.3 Proactive and reactive approaches

Getting the message out doesn't end, of course, when a news segment ends. Many listeners, viewers, and digital users will continue the conversation. They will comment on social media, some even in person to friends and colleagues, about what they have learned and how it affected them.

And like the ripple effect from a drop of water, the news lives on.

What if My Audience Is Not Global? Or National?

You don't have to be the size of BP or Maple Leaf Foods to need—and benefit from—a solid media relations plan. In fact, if you have a social media presence, or if you have a website, you have a media presence.

We discuss audiences later in the book, but for now let's focus on the idea that follower or stakeholder size is not the driving factor. It's about impact, not numbers. You are better off to get your message to 50 people who are interested in what you have to say, to offer, or to sell than you are to reach 500 people who do not want to do a downward dog with dachshunds (more about this later in Chapter 4). When you have content—something you want to say—and you feel mainstream and social media will help you disseminate this message, then you are engaging in media relations. The key is to be strategic and thoughtful about this engagement.

That thoughtfulness—and strategic thinking—extends to your own digital space. This virtual messaging is a resource and a record. It can help reporters with fact checking, further engage interested parties, and may even help to balance perceptions of your organization.

What Does Media Relations Have to Do with Communications and Marketing?

Everything. Communications, often called public relations, builds sustained and substantive relationships with key audiences or stakeholders. Many organizations have communications departments, communications plans, and communications policies that guide their interactions with customers, supporters, voters, donors, and other users of their services.

For those with communications structures in place, media will be a key audience, and media relations will play an integral part in their outreach efforts. The same is true for marketing departments and campaigns. Media relations can complement these initiatives. It certainly did for Red Bull.

Case Study

Red Bull Stratos

Red Bull wanted to go where no human had gone before, and as it turned out, where no business had gone before. With its campaign Red Bull Stratos, the energy-drink company dared to pull off the world's highest-altitude jump. On October 14, 2012, Felix Baumgartner did just that. As the world watched, the Austrian skydiver rose 24 miles above the clouds hanging from a helium balloon. Then he let go. For the first time in history, the sound barrier was broken without help from an engine.

Other records were shattered as well. According to YouTube, the jump was viewed live by more than eight million people, making it then the most-watched livestream ever. But it wasn't only livestreaming and social media that skyrocketed. Forty TV network stations and 130 digital outlets covered the event.

In her report *Red Bull Stratos: Public Relations Case Study*, Allison Melrose highlights the use of traditional, or earned, media that Red Bull included as part of its daredevil campaign. The company "did an excellent job of communicating with journalists before, during, and after the event to gain third-party credibility," she noted, adding that one of the key ways Red Bull communicated was through the online Red Bull Stratos Newsroom it created on their media relations website, Red Bull Content Pool. Here reporters could quickly and easily access mission information, fact sheets, and photos.

"This is an excellent way to control the message about the campaign and disseminate information to a large number of journalists," Melrose concluded. How did she reach this conclusion? "This method clearly worked, as all earned media mentioned Red Bull. Journalists could have easily dropped the 'Red Bull' in 'Red Bull Stratos,' but the company made their role in the event so integral that the media left it in."

And that is media relations. Of course, things could have gone terribly wrong and that would have resulted in many stories of a very different tone and tenor. Planning reduces these risks and enhances the rewards.

CHAPTER 2

Have We Got News for You

"Bad news isn't wine. It doesn't improve with age."
—Colin Powell, Former U.S. Secretary of State

All the News That's Fit to Print

We talk about news as if it's one thing. Did you hear the news? According to the news…. It was in the news. News isn't one thing. It is many things. In particular, it is two things: hard, soft.

Hard news is often what draws us in and keeps us reading, listening, and watching. You'll find it on the front page, at the start of a newscast, and at the top of the hour. Hard news is big news: controversy and crisis. It is immediate, and it is important. It's often called "breaking news."

The AAFT School of Journalism and Mass Communication notes that

Hard news serves as the backbone of an informed society, providing critical information about significant events that shape our world…. The urgency and objectivity inherent in hard news reporting contribute to a well-informed public discourse, holding leaders accountable and fostering a foundation for democratic societies.

Soft news does not send us scrambling. It is the intersection between information and entertainment. It is not usually immediate—you can learn about the signs of stroke or how to make an easy apple pie without apples at any point in time—and it is increasingly about personalities, famous and otherwise.

As AAFT points out, "In a world where information overload is common, soft news offers a refreshing break, catering to diverse interests and enriching the news landscape with stories about lifestyle, culture, sports, and human-interest narratives."

Many companies have carved a niche in the soft news market. Dove, for example, is known for its "Real Beauty" campaign, which uses social media and other media platforms to promote body positivity and self-acceptance, going beyond traditional product marketing. Airbnb, Inc., uses social media and its blog to share stories about travel, local culture, and the experiences its platform facilitates, reinforcing its brand values and creating a sense of community.

To show you the difference between hard and soft news, take a look at the difference between these headlines in Figure 2.1.

Differentiating Hard News and Soft News

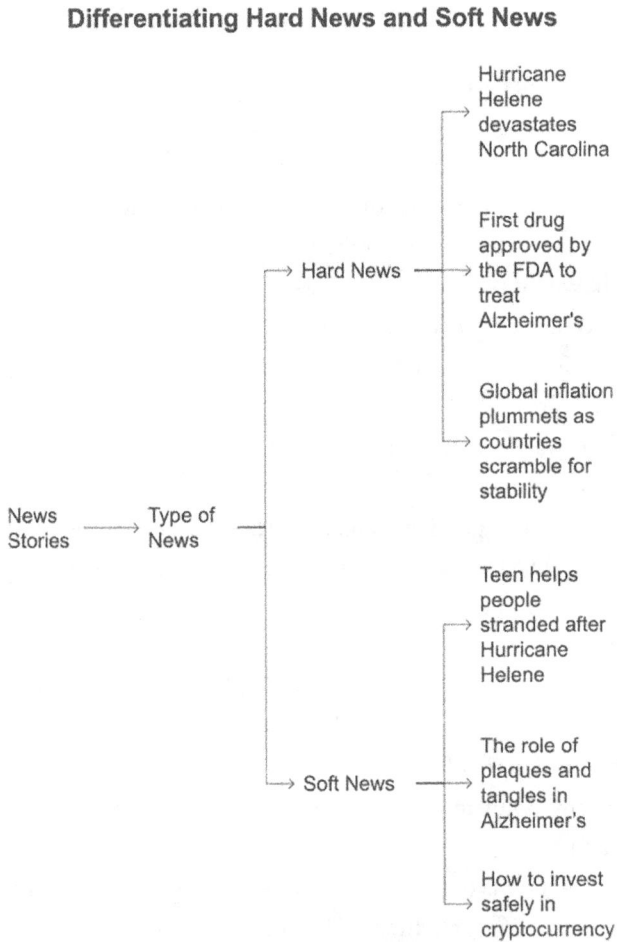

Figure 2.1 *Finding differences between hard and soft news*

Topics and timeliness are only two of the distinctions that serve to classify news as hard or soft. How the story is told also differs. Hard news almost invariably starts up front with the "headline" then provides the details to flesh out the headline. Soft news has more options; it can be more creative and more flexible in its structure and content.

Objectivity is another distinguishing feature. Journalists report on hard news. They require sources, usually at least two to confirm facts. They do not offer commentary or opinions. That is the domain of soft news. In keeping with the landscapes in which they operate, hard news has that edge to it. It sounds professional, even formal. Authoritative and accurate. Soft news is often more casual and conversational. It can be relaxing, funny, interesting without being heavy.

There is a final distinction between hard and soft news that is important: shelf life. Hard news breaks. It dominates. Then it moves on to the next issue of importance. Soft news can hang around for a while, it lingers. Its relevancy has greater longevity in part because much of the information it contains is unlikely to change, unlike hard news. Think about the reporting on COVID-19, which was evolving on a daily basis, versus an article on how to reduce heartburn.

Many of the companies, nonprofits, and government departments that shy away from an active media relations program often do so because they don't want to land on the front page or be the lead in the evening news. But this is hard news, and hard news is inevitably linked to bad news, at the very least, controversial or contentious news.

Media relations prepares your organization for hard-news stories that may break and involve you, but this is not its focus. It is focused on soft news: general interest and lifestyle. It is about getting the stories out there that speak to the work that you do and the organization that you are. It's about building your voice so that when you do speak, credibility shines through.

Of course, there is more than news, of any type. There is opinion, commentary, editorials, podcasts, and more. Bloggers and influencers often work in these realms. More and more writers with a background in journalism are using these mediums to go beyond reporting, and some platforms such as Substack offer a high degree of credibility and reach. They should be considered when you are charting your media relations plan.

News Elements

Three main criteria define hard news.

1. Timeliness

   When a hurricane rages, a groundbreaking new drug is approved, the economy is getting pummeled, the news media rush to report on these events as they are unfolding.

   Once unfolded, these stories move to the backburner. However, they may have spinoffs that make their way into the lifestyle pages, health news, and human-interest stories. These are stories often more difficult for reporters, bloggers, and influencers to find because they do not dominate the news, or even social media, and sources are not always obvious or easy to find.

2. Grandeur. Hard news is also big news

   The fifty-sixth drug to be approved for the treatment of warts does not lead off the six o'clock broadcast or top Facebook News. It is unlikely to garner much, if any, coverage. On the other hand, newly published research indicating that the cause of attention deficit hyperactivity disorder (ADHD) has been discovered will be widely reported on in mainstream media and specialized outlets, including those focused on medicine, education, families, and the pharmaceutical sector.

   "Big" is also relative. When Queen Elizabeth II died, her death was reported around the world, including in countries that are not part of the British Commonwealth. When Mae*Zing Grace died, no one reported on it, although donalee was devastated, and the vet's office sent a lovely card saying the little cat would be missed. (She still is.)

   The significance of a story is linked to the third element in hard news.

3. Relevance

Relevance is linked to timeliness—and geography. If McDonald's Corporation were to announce it was closing all its fast-food outlets worldwide, there would be a global rush to report on the announcement. If Tavern on the Green, in New York's Central Park, revealed it was shuttering its doors after 90 years, NY radio, television, online, and print outlets would carry the story. If Lou's Pizza, the oldest eatery in Boonville, Missouri, was unable to make ends meet and had to declare the family-owned business bankrupt, the *Boonville Missouri News* would run the story on its front page. The *St. Louis Post-Dispatch* might run a small item on an inside page.

The elements that define hard news—timely, big, relevant—also apply to soft news when it comes to media relations and pitching stories that an organization wants to see garner media coverage. For example, if your company has manufactured the fifty-sixth drug to be approved for the treatment of warts, sending out a news release in August to national media is likely a waste of time and money. You could get clever, however. As Halloween approaches, you could reach out to news outlets with the pitch that witches this year will no longer arrive on doorsteps sporting warts—thanks to your company's new FDA-approved treatment.

You could also get strategic.

If mainstream media is unlikely to pick up your story because it is not "news," bypass the mainstream and seek out specialized outlets for whom the information would be timely and relevant. If the treatment requires a prescription, pitch to *Skin Healthy Magazine*, published by the American Academy of Dermatology Association. If no prescription is required, try *Pharmacy Times*.

Cardinal Rule #1:
If you have no news, don't go to the media.

Cardinal Rule #2:
The fact that you are a good organization with good services or products is not news.

Today's News Context

The discussion so far has presumed media follow traditional rules of journalism, which call for impartiality, fairness, and balance. In many countries, many outlets have shifted away from this type of reporting, and there may be media relations advantages for your organization with these outlets.

According to the 2019 report *News in a Digital Age: Comparing the Presentation of News Information over Time and Across Media Platforms* by Jennifer Kavanagh et al., news content has generally shifted from more-objective event- and context-based reporting to reporting that is more subjective, relies more heavily on argumentation and advocacy, and includes more emotional appeals. "These changes were observed across platforms, appearing least significant in the evolution of print journalism and most stark in comparisons of broadcast news with prime-time cable programming and of print journalism with online journalism."

But old-school journalism still carries a punch, however. A 2021 study, *The Relevance of Impartial News in a Polarised World: A report by JV Consulting* commissioned by the Reuters Institute for the Study of Journalism, University of Oxford, found that impartiality—along with accuracy—remains a bedrock of trust in the news media. The survey, conducted in four countries, including the United States and the UK, is focused more on traditional reporting of hard news, but hard news is the foundation on which soft news flourishes, and traditional reporting is what gives organizations credibility when their stories are carried by mainstream news outlets.

Warts and all.

CHAPTER 3

Inside the Modern Newsroom

"The pessimist complains about the wind; the optimist expects it to change; the realist adjusts the sails."

—William Arthur Ward, American Writer

Once upon a time, in a land not so far away from today, people started their morning ritual drinking a cup of coffee and reading the newspaper. The newspaper was printed on paper, usually a broadsheet, 12 in. (305 mm) wide by 22.75 in. (578 mm) long. On the front page was harder-hitting news of significance locally, nationally, internationally. Inside were sports, entertainment news, local stories, classified advertisements. There was even a whole page devoted to comics and at least one to obituaries. Everywhere there were ads.

Before the Internet, mobile devices, and social media, newspapers were thick and robust, at least in heft. According to the Guinness World Records, the most massive single issue of a newspaper was the September 13, 1987 Sunday edition of *The New York Times*, which weighed more than 5.4 kg (12 lb) and contained 1,612 pages.

Those people who once upon a time started their day reading the newspaper often ended it by tuning into the news—on television. In 1980, according to the Pew Research Center, 52.1 million Americans watched the evening news.

Times have changed. Newspaper circulation dipped ten percent in the 1980s and 1990s, and it continues to fall steadily today although not in double-digit territory. TV news has suffered a similar fate. In his article "As Evening TV News Shows Resume Their Decline, Some Suggestions from a Text Guy," Richard Tofel notes, "…where nearly one in four Americans (including children) watched an evening network news broadcast in 1980, that proportion had collapsed to fewer than one in 14 in 2019."

Clearly times have changed. And yet, much has remained the same. In 2023, *The New York Times* had 296,330 print subscribers, making it the second-largest newspaper in the United States. Still a popular read. *The Times* is more popular online, however, with 8.83 million subscribers—more than any other newspaper in the United States.

TV news is also popular, but the demographic is skewed. According to research from the Pew Research Center, in 2022, adults aged 50 and above were the primary viewers of local TV news, with nearly 65 percent watching it regularly. This needs to be put into context, of course. Today, digital devices are by far the most common way Americans get news.

This shifting landscape has significant implications for media relations. To respond effectively to the current media environment, we need to understand how today's newsroom operates, the constraints reporters and outlets face, and the opportunities a new media world opens up.

Inside the Modern Newsroom

Television shows and movies have portrayed newsrooms as bustling places where journalists, editors, and interns jostle to finish stories on deadline or get breaking news to the anchor desk before airtime. There is a thread of truth that runs throughout these fictional scenes. It took a lot of talented people to get a newspaper into the hands of readers nationally and locally. It took a lot of talented people to beam the nightly news into homes across a country, a community.

The modern newsroom is smaller. There is less bustle because there are significantly fewer people reporting on the news, hard or soft, and there are fewer people turning to traditional media to stay informed. The Brookings Institution, for example, reports that the number of journalists at U.S. newspapers dropped 39 percent between 1989 and 2012 alone, from 59,000 to 36,000. Reductions continue. In January 2024, the *Los Angeles Times* cut its newsroom staff by 20 percent. It was not alone.

To a large extent, the diminished newsroom size reflects diminished advertising revenue. A U.S. Census Bureau survey found that newspapers made roughly $22.1 billion in revenue in 2020—less than half what they made in 2002. Fewer sales means belt tightening.

It also means pivoting.

More and more people are turning to social media and online news to keep abreast of what is happening close to home and further away. A 2010 survey conducted by the Pew Internet and American Life Project found that 61 percent of Americans got at least some of their news online. Less than a decade later, Facebook, Inc. announced the launch of Facebook News.

The Way We Are

Times have changed. Online sources have opened up a new and often affordable world for individuals looking to access information and contribute to the information age. Mainstream media formats are no longer considered essential by many even if they are still primary sources of information for some.

The move to digital has had significant implications for journalists and other information providers. Speed is of the essence. This means, on the one hand, we get news more quickly and get to keep up to date on issues as they emerge and as they change. On the other hand, speed also means errors, confusion, corrections. Audiences are suspect. The Reuters Institute 2024 Digital News Report found that concern about accuracy had risen globally three percentage points in the past year to 59 percent. The level of concern is even higher in the United States at 72 percent.

Digital media is also global media. Events happening around the world are reported on with the same speed as local news. We no longer wait for news from overseas. It is only a click away.

This often means digital media is using information, photos, and links from mainstream, or legacy, media. Digital media may do less actual reporting and more distributing. When you're considering where to pitch, consider that.

The demand for immediacy—and the expectation that this demand will be met—has put pressure on journalists and others to report quickly, often at breakneck speed. There is equal pressure to report over diverse media. Journalists covering a trial, for instance, will be expected to tweet about events, post updates, take pics, and perhaps even offer commentary. One journalist we know remembered with dismay ducking out of a courtroom to post something on the media outlet's socials only to return and discover a key piece of evidence had been introduced in their absence.

The new world of media is a new world for those reporting on it as well.

Another major change is the move from specialist to generalist. For larger media outlets, it was common to have reporters dedicated to sports, movies, entertainment, politics. They got to know these sectors and could report authoritatively. Today, specialization has given way to generalization for many media, including larger companies. This means a journalist may be reporting on a medical breakthrough on Monday, the verdict in a criminal trial on Tuesday, and puppy yoga on Wednesday.

Fewer reporters, camera operators, editors, producers, production staff means a new way of working for many. Reporters now often do their own camera work. One TV morning show we are familiar with has no camera operator at all. Instead, a stationary camera is set up in one specific location and all interviews are conducted from behind a desk. Another brings a smartphone with him to conduct interviews by setting the phone up and pressing record.

Those being interviewed are limited in what they can show and do without stepping outside stationary camera range.

Implications for Media Relations

The new way of working has significant implications for media relations—for getting your news into a newsroom and out into the world. Fewer reporters mean fewer people to contact, fewer people to read a release or hear a pitch. You will have to work harder—and more strategically—to get your pitch heard. To get a yes.

Fewer reporters also mean less likelihood a reporter, photographer and/or camera operator will be able to travel any distance to cover your story. Interviews may be remotely done via phone or Zoom. You may find yourself in an empty room with only a camera. The reporter is in a studio on the other side of the state or the country.

That distance has implications for the connection you'd like to establish with media and the depth of the story. It will be important to become comfortable with the technology and take the extra step to provide background information and images. It is also important to consider how you want to appear. What is behind you? Where is the light source? Where is your camera? (Nose hairs are never attractive.)

The digital world has also impacted the way we pitch stories. News releases, which highlighted the story at the top and included details and quotes as you continued reading, are quickly becoming a thing of the past. Media advisories alerting reporters to events and opportunities are also used less frequently. This is a nod to technology that lets us get our ideas into the hands of reporters, bloggers, and influencers in a myriad of ways.

It is also a reflection that attention spans have declined. In his 2024 article in *PRNews*, "How PR and Media Relations Have Changed in the Past Decade," Gabriel de la Rosa points out that there is demand for shorter content. "Years ago, published articles sometimes reached 1,500 to 1,700 words. Over time the typical word count dropped to 1,200, then 1,000, and nowadays, you can regularly find articles in high-tier publications that are just 800 words."

The reduction, de la Rosa says, is linked to something else that has declined: our attention span, now reportedly less than half as long as it was a decade ago. What's a savvy organization to do? Go with the times. Make sure your story is interesting. Make sure it's relevant. Get to the point.

AI—The New Kid in the Class

There is a new reality in the newsroom and in media relations: AI. Artificial intelligence can be a boon to your media relations program. And it can be a detriment.

On the plus side, AI can do a lot of the grunt work. If you want to reach media, you need to know how to reach them. That's called a media list, and it is a pain to update. Yet updated it must be. AI relishes this type of task and does it within minutes if not seconds. That frees up time for your team to spend elsewhere on less routine tasks.

AI can help to make stories shorter, more concise, even change the tone.

Artificial intelligence chatbots like ChatGPT and Microsoft's Copilot enable organizations to quickly edit, create, and revise. What it doesn't do is remove the need for a human writer. And that isn't bias talking. It's fact.

AI can tell you how to say something. It cannot tell you what you want to say. And it cannot replace the people who decide what their story needs, how it will impact specific audiences, and how it will move your organization closer to its media (and other) goals. AI is the intern that needs to be shown the ropes but is far from ready to lead the way.

The use of AI to write pitches, releases and more can be problematic. First, it may be treated as spam by many media outlets, which means your pitch never makes it to any person let alone the right person.

The use of AI to pitch story ideas and experts in your organization is efficient, but it is machine driven. That flies in the face of Media Relations 101: Establishing a Relationship with the Media. If you'd like AI to create social media posts, write pitches, and draft releases, treat that as a starting point. Then bring in a human touch.

The use of AI is all about balance. It provides opportunities not known before it began to take hold of our world in its current form. But it needs to be accepted and appreciated as a tool, not the mastermind.

The way we were

"The post-war American newsroom resembled a vast factory churning out multiple editions through the night. Reporters spent days, sometimes weeks, on a single story." —Lionel Barber, U.K. journalist

CHAPTER 4

Getting Inside Your Audiences

"Content is only king when people actually want to read it."

—Adam Davis, Former Marketing
Content Manager, Arbox Ltd.

The human communications process has four broad components: sender, message, medium, and receiver (Figure 4.1).

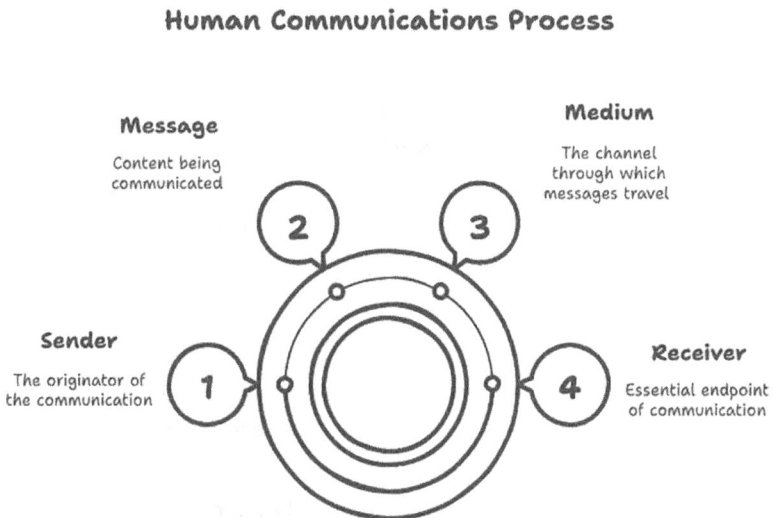

Human Communications Process

Message
Content being communicated

Medium
The channel through which messages travel

Sender
The originator of the communication

Receiver
Essential endpoint of communication

2 3

1 4

Figure 4.1 Human communications process

The process appears quite simple. It's anything but. The elements of the process, however, can be summarized simply. Someone has to be able to say something, to have something to say, and to have a way to say it. Then someone has to receive the message.

In other words, no receiver, no message.

While each element in the communications process is important, one outranks all the others. The receiver is #1. You tailor your message to the person or people who need to get your message or will benefit the most from it. Otherwise, you waste your time, money, and effort. You also just might annoy your receivers and hurt your reputation.

For example, we just received an e-mail promoting a new yoga class—with dachshunds! Count us in. We love puppies and yoga, and we are willing to pay for the privilege of doing a downward dog with a dog. Well-targeted message.

Almost. When we eagerly read the e-mail for registration details, we discovered the one-day-only class was in a city almost 900 miles away from where we live. We were disappointed to learn this opportunity wasn't intended for us, and frustrated we received the message anyway.

On Target

In media relations, the term "audience" has two meanings. It refers to those people you want to reach with your messaging so they will know more about your product, service, or issue. This is one type of target audience.

A second target audience is the media outlets themselves, the reporters, the bloggers, the influencers who report on the sector or industry you work in. You are better identifying who is likely to be interested in your pitch than sending it to everyone you can find and frustrating them. Frustrate media enough and they will stop paying attention when you reach out.

Identifying audiences can be tricky—and painstaking. Audiences are broken down into four key categories: primary, secondary, external, and internal. The first three have direct relevance to media relations. The fourth should not be overlooked.

Primary audiences are your main target. These are the people who will directly benefit from your message or have an interest in your product, service, or issue. Secondary audiences, on the other hand, are those people for whom your information will be nice to know but not essential.

External audiences are your customers, your supporters, your donors, your stakeholders. Internal audiences are employees, who are often overlooked.

Let's try our hand at audience analysis. Let's imagine we work for RenewSkin Sciences, which has just had a new treatment approved for the safe and effective removal of warts. We want to tell the world. But we're smarter than that. All the world is not interested in warts.

Who is? People who have warts. Yep. But how do we find them? Well, they go to family doctors, specialists, and pharmacists. They sure do, and those professionals have associations. Those associations have conferences. People with health issues also often have support groups and Facebook groups. And this is just the tip of the iceberg.

On the media side, health care professions usually have trade publications, online and in print. This might be an issue parents are also interested in, and there are lots of publications and blogs aimed at parents. More general media often run lifestyle pieces or health stories. Warts have gotten a bad rap. We can use this.

The key is to dig down. Be specific. For example, it is not enough to say people with warts often go to the doctor. What type of doctor? Family physicians. Dermatologists. Not OB-GYNs. (That is a different kind of wart.)

Once you have narrowed down the audience, you can begin to identify the media affiliated with them and start to build a database of contacts. In some cases, you will reach your intended audience directly. In other cases, you will reach them indirectly. Regardless, you will reach them.

Media relations is focused on reaching outside your organization to audiences and individuals who may not know who you are or what you do, may not know you well, or may not be aware of your latest news. External audiences, especially media, usually do not share your expertise and even when they do, they may not share your specific point of view. How you provide information will be critical, and we'll discuss this later in the book.

For now, let's look inward. Internal audiences are often ignored in media relations because the focus is on reaching out. But it is important to engage and inform internal audiences for two important reasons. One, you don't want them to feel left out. There is nothing more demoralizing for employees than to read something about their organization in the media that the organization originated—and employees weren't aware of it until an "outsider" told them.

Employees are also boosters of the organizations they work for. They share information with others, they post and repost on socials, they support the work you do and speak to its quality. It's important to bring them in and, in doing so, demonstrate that they are valued. Depending on the reason your organization will be in the news, offer them key messages or seek input on how they would like to help boost the messages you want to deliver.

The key to effective audience analysis is time. Take time to reflect on what it is you have to say and who needs to hear this. Start broadly and drill down. Be as specific as possible. And be rigorous. Don't include someone simply because the technology makes it easy to reach a thousand people even though only one hundred are truly primary audiences. Be strategic and you will be successful.

CHAPTER 5

There Oughta Be a Policy

"Policies are many, Principles are few, Policies will change, Principles never do."

—John C. Maxwell, Author of *The 21 Irrefutable Laws of Leadership*

Media relations requires a framework. While you can write pitches, identify opportunities, and distribute releases ad hoc, these tasks are best performed within the context of an overarching policy. This policy clarifies the relationship you want to have with media and why that relationship matters. It sets out who speaks to the media, when you speak to the media as an organization, how you speak to the media, and maybe even where you speak to the media. It also emphasizes what it is you want to say.

Here's what the media policy doesn't do: spell out specifics about how you will reach out to media over the course of a year, what tactics you will use, or what goals you will seek to attain. That's all in the media relations plan, and that is in the next chapter.

Let's start our foray into media policies by looking at two actual examples: the U.S. Department of Health & Human Services (HHS) and the City of Sault Ste. Marie, Ontario. The full text of each policy is available in Appendix A and Appendix B, respectively. These media policies will help to give you a sense of how organizations conceive of media relations and how they take that higher-level thinking and transform it into a policy.

We're going to take a high-level look and a quick comparison.

Figure 5.1 shows the seven sections in the 2022 HHS policy.

By contrast, Figure 5.2 shows Sault Ste. Marie's policy with 17 sections.

The overlap and the differences are apparent—and important. A media policy must reflect the needs and expectations of your organization.

HHS Policy Components

Background	Purpose and Scope	Responsibilities	Guidelines
Media Procedures	Personal Media Procedures	Social Media Procedures	

Figure 5.1 Seven components in HHS policy

Sault Ste. Marie Policy Components

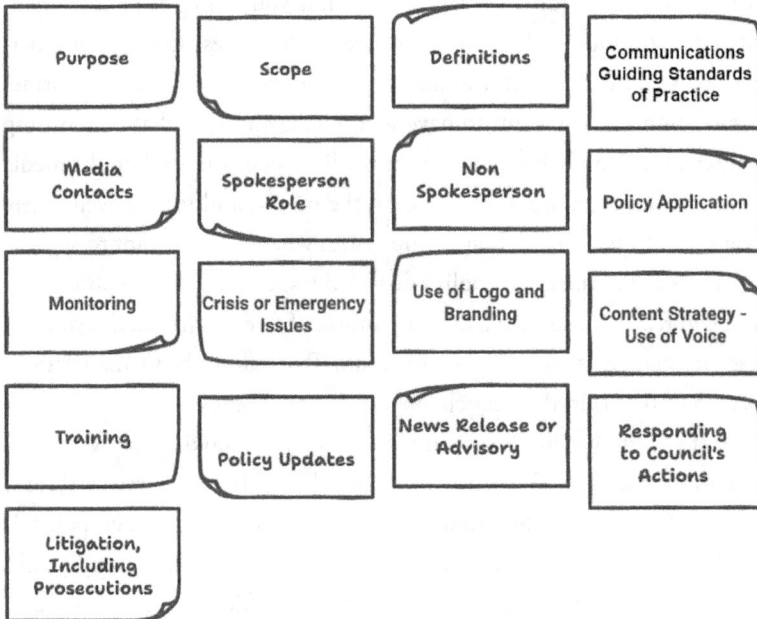

Purpose	Scope	Definitions	Communications Guiding Standards of Practice
Media Contacts	Spokesperson Role	Non Spokesperson	Policy Application
Monitoring	Crisis or Emergency Issues	Use of Logo and Branding	Content Strategy – Use of Voice
Training	Policy Updates	News Release or Advisory	Responding to Council's Actions
Litigation, Including Prosecutions			

Figure 5.2 Sault Ste. Marie's 17 policy components

While a template or a little help from AI to get started makes sense, you will need to determine the relationship you want to have as an organization with the media and how to build that relationship.

The HHS policy (as of April 3, 2025) is founded on a commitment to "a culture of openness with the media and public that values the free exchange of ideas, data, and information and doing so in a manner that is timely, responsive, and accurate."

As seen in its 2017 "Purpose" statement, the City of Sault Ste. Marie takes a different approach, and tone, but there is a shared understanding that media relations is a two-way endeavor.

> A strategic approach to media relations is required to build an equally beneficial and trusting relationship with news media in order to foster accurate and fair reporting; increase positive news coverage; and protect and enhance the City's reputation and integrity.

This two-way understanding must be more than lip service. Reporters, bloggers, and influencers are intelligent and savvy. If there is nothing in the relationship for them, there is no relationship.

Sault Ste. Marie identifies five guiding standards of practice. Among them are three that speak directly to the collaborative relationship they want with media, the commitment to a symmetrical approach, and the value they place on ensuring employees are among the first to know:

1. Work collaboratively to respond to all media queries in a timely way. This may include media contacts outside traditional office hours or days of work.
2. Communications prepared by the Corporation conform to professional journalistic practices and standards in terms of style, content, and timing, and will support two-way symmetrical communication engagement opportunities with the media.
3. The Corporation recognizes that Council and staff should have the opportunity to learn about major developments from the Corporation first. Accordingly, efforts will be taken to post news releases and messages appropriately.

HHS does not have guiding standards of practice set out in its media relations policy, but it does have eight core communications principles that apply across the organization. Half of them address the value of timeliness and relevance as well as respect for the reader in ensuring plain language principles are upheld.

1. Be honest and accurate in all communications.
2. Respond promptly to media requests and respect media deadlines.
3. Promote plain writing of media documents and releases.
4. Create greatest transparency possible through distributing information timely and widely through Internet, e-mail, media wires, and other mechanisms.

In addition to identifying the foundation on which your policy is built and the approach your organization takes, your media relations policy should include guidance regarding who may be spokespeople. Who can speak on behalf of the organization? Who cannot? Is there a process that should be followed when approached by media?

HHS notes that "while speaking to the media is not a requirement, employees are encouraged to speak to reporters about their work whenever possible and appropriate." When approached by a reporter, the policy states, "HHS employees should work with their immediate supervisor and coordinate with the appropriate public affairs office/personnel in their agency."

This form of guidance may generate the need for/interest in media training. However, it establishes a sense of transparency within the organization in that the messaging isn't being contained or controlled centrally.

The City of Sault Ste. Marie has another, equally valid, process, one that applies a limit on who can and should speak. This doesn't mean that transparency isn't valued. It may mean that their media relations strategy is to ensure impact, timeliness, and that it is used to support specific goals and objectives.

The Corporate Communications Officer or City Clerk is the designated management contact for media activity, whether initiated by the City or by media outlets. The centralization of this role ensures consistency and responsiveness. Any employee who receives media calls or requests for information should refer them to the Corporate Communications Officer or City Clerk for processing.

While adding one more policy to the already burgeoning collection of policies should not be done without care and thought, a media relations policy plays an important role in your relationship with media. The purpose is to ensure consistency of message when speaking with media and enhance efficiency through the use of a clear process. This helps to eliminate confusion internally and add polish to your reputation professionally.

CHAPTER 6

Plan on It

"First comes thought; then organization of that thought, into ideas and plans; then transformation of those plans into reality."

—Napoleon Hill, Author of *Think and Grow Rich*

Effective media relations activities don't just happen. They're planned and that planning starts with an overarching media relations policy.

Building a successful media relations plan requires groundwork. You will need to set strategic goals, identify "news" within your organization and how to share it, and develop a media kit. Media relations plans also often identify action items for the year, provide a to-do checklist, help generate ideas to build ongoing media awareness, and provide key messages. In addition, there may be smaller, targeted plans prepared for special events, announcements, and opportunities.

A standard media relations plan, as illustrated in Figure 6.1, requires you, at a minimum, to address the following:

- State your goal.
- Create your proposition statement.
- Have clear objectives for media coverage.
- Define desired reach.
- Establish frequency.
- Ensure continuity.

Additionally, the plan may highlight research that needs to be conducted; identify target audiences and participant communities; provide profiles of your audiences; and include a call to action.

You should also create an inventory of assets, like experts and resources, that you can call upon when opportunity knocks.

There's more.

Standard Media Relations Planning Funnel

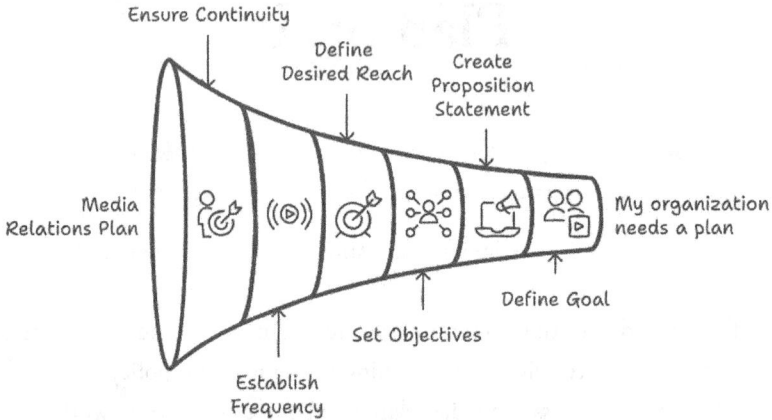

Figure 6.1 Standard communications funnel

Your media relations plan will identify necessary resources; set a budget; highlight format, tactics, tools; create a timeline; and evaluate outcomes and measure your impact.

Although the best media relations plan will be the plan that works for your organization and is tailored to meet your needs, Figure 6.2 illustrates an approach that broadens the one demonstrated in Figure 6.1.

- Situational Analysis
- Goal
- Objectives
- Target Audience
- Strategy Development
- Key Messages
- Story Angles
- Tactics
- Media List

Let's try our hand at developing a high-level media relations plan for RenewSkin Sciences, our wonderful wart company with a newly approved product, WartX.

Strategic Communication Planning Funnel

Goal Setting
Defining the desired outcome

Objective Formulation
Establishing measurable steps

Target Audience Identification
Identifying the intended recipients

Strategy Development
Creating a comprehensive plan

Key Message Crafting
Developing core communication points

Story Angle Creation
Finding compelling narratives

Tactical Implementation
Executing specific actions

Figure 6.2 Broad strategic communications funnel

Situational Analysis (your current landscape)
RenewSkin Sciences, a national dermatological company, has received U.S. Food & Drug Administration (FDA) approval for WartX, a new treatment designed for the safe and effective removal of warts. The treatment is an advance in the field and positions the company as a leader in skincare solutions. However, there is little awareness of WartX among the public, and health care professionals are not switching from their traditional treatments. Media engagement is crucial to inform target audiences, build credibility, and establish RenewSkin Sciences as a trusted name in dermatology.

Goal (your broad, general aim)
To raise greater awareness about WartX, specifically and more generally establish RenewSkin Sciences as a leading innovator in dermatological treatments.

Objectives (how you'll know you've succeeded specifically and measurably)

- Reach: Ensure WartX benefits are communicated to at least 70 percent of the target audience within six months.
- Frequency: Generate at least 12 media mentions in reputable health and lifestyle outlets during the first quarter.
- Continuity: Maintain consistent media coverage by securing at least one feature or news mention per month over the next year.

Target Audiences (those you need to reach)
Primary audiences:

- Dermatologists
- Family doctors
- Nurse practitioners
- Patients suffering from warts
- Parents of kids with warts
- School nurses
- Health and science journalists
- Pharmacists
- Dermatology conference organizers

Secondary audiences (those it's nice to reach)

- Medical school students
- Health care students
- Medical and health care associations

Strategy Development (your approach to garnering increased awareness)

- Show how the treatment is a breakthrough using stories and data.

- Build relationships with key media outlets and journalists specializing in health, science, and lifestyle.
- Spotlight the expertise of RenewSkin Sciences' leadership team, health experts, and researchers.

Key Messages (what you want people to remember)

- WartX is a safe, effective, and easy solution for wart removal.
- WartX is a breakthrough in wart treatment.
- Living with warts is not painless. Removing them can be.

Story Angles (how you will focus your media materials)

- The science behind the treatment's efficacy and safety profile
- Patient success stories and testimonials
- RenewSkin Sciences' journey through the research and approval process
- Expert interviews with researchers and dermatologists

Tactics (what you will do)

1. Media Outreach
   - Distribute a press release announcing approval of the new treatment.
   - Schedule interviews with RenewSkin Sciences' CEO and lead researchers.
   - Pitch story ideas targeted to health, science, and lifestyle media outlets.
   - Offer guests for call-in radio shows, which have a voracious appetite for content.
2. Content Creation
   - Develop a comprehensive media kit, including:
     - Company backgrounder
     - Treatment fact sheet
     - Expert bios

- High-resolution images
- FAQs
  - Create engaging multimedia content such as explainer videos and infographics.
3. Event Management
   - Host a virtual or in-person press conference to showcase the launch of WartX.
   - Organize webinars featuring dermatology experts discussing wart treatment advancements.
4. Social Media and Digital Campaigns
   - Amplify key messages through RenewSkin Sciences' social media platforms.
   - Collaborate with influencers in dermatology and skincare niches.
5. Community Engagement
   - Partner with dermatology clinics and maybe beauty schools to provide information sessions.
   - Offer free samples or discounts through medical professionals to encourage patient trials.

Media List Development (who you need to reach in the media)

- Identify and maintain a comprehensive list of:
  - Health and science journalists from major publications such as Healthline, Medscape, WebMD, and *The New York Times*
  - Editors of dermatology-focused journals
  - Editors of family medicine journals
  - Influencers in the skincare and health sectors
  - Local and national broadcast media contacts

Resources and Budget

Resources

- Dedicated media relations person or team
- Media monitoring tools
- Graphic design and media distribution services, if necessary

Budget

- Allocate funding for:
  - Media kit production
  - Event hosting
  - Digital advertising
  - Print ads
  - Influencer partnerships

Timeline

1. Month 1
   - Finalize media kit and press release.
   - Host news conference, if desired.
   - Begin outreach to top-tier journalists and outlets.
   - Launch social media teaser campaign.
2. Months 2 to 3
   - Arrange interviews and secure media placements.
   - Host webinar.
3. Months 4 to 6
   - Maintain outreach momentum with monthly pitches.
   - Roll out patient-focused campaigns.
4. Months 7 to 12
   - Evaluate progress through a number of tools, including media reach and coverage.
   - Adjust strategy as needed.
   - Focus on continuity with long-term media relationships.

Evaluation and Impact Measurement

- Track media mentions and audit content.
- Measure social media engagement metrics.
- Assess audience reach through impressions and viewership statistics.
- Collect feedback from stakeholders, including journalists and health care professionals, as appropriate.

This "plan," of course, is only a starting point. It represents initial and high-level thinking. From here, it will need to be fleshed out, expanded, and shared for comment.

Like all plans, it must be flexible. As circumstances change, as opportunities arise, as feedback filters in, the plan will be adjusted. New ideas and information will be added, existing approaches and tactics revised or dropped.

All this is required because effective media relations doesn't just happen. It's planned.

CHAPTER 7

Mastering Media Interviews

"Publicity is absolutely critical. A good PR story is infinitely more effective than a front page ad."

—Richard Branson, founder of the Virgin Group

There can be no media relations without speaking to the media. This requires more than opening one's mouth and hearing words come out. Indeed, that can be a recipe for disaster.

Many organizations are worried that the media will "twist" what they're saying or take information "out of context." As media relations professionals, we are more worried that spokespeople will wing it and ramble along. Or they will prove their expertise and use a language, complete with alphabet soup, that most readers and listeners will not understand. There is no faster way to bore people, confuse people, and drive them somewhere else than using elevated language, providing irrelevant information, and focusing on you instead of your audience.

Some will suggest you need to "dumb it down." This is false. The onus is not the sole responsibility of the reader or listener to understand what you are saying. If you are an IT professional, you may use language with your colleagues that those who are not in the industry don't understand. This is not because they are dumb, it's because they went to school or built their expertise in an entirely different area.

Using plain language to communicate is a sign of well thought-out, well-established messaging that respects the reader. It's a sign of an organization that wants the reader to get the messages it's conveying.

Once the messaging has been established, working with your spokespeople to be comfortable on camera is next.

Being comfortable on camera, relaxed when a microphone is placed in front of you, and able to clearly articulate responses to an array of questions rarely comes without help. Most people haven't been trained to appear confident and comfortable, formally or informally. Formal media training can come internally or with help from external experts. Informal can merely be a discussion and a quick run through of tips.

Either way, media training helps prepare spokespeople for interviews they've requested—and those they haven't. It's about understanding the process and preparing to deliver your message as professionally as possible.

It's also about understanding the landscape. The fact is, most interviews are not confrontational. Indeed, they are usually professional and informative.

Two, sometimes divergent, factors are at play: what's in this for your audience (i.e., why should they pay attention) and what do you want the audience to know about your organization, your product, or your service.

It's critical to understand how to hold attention and how to get your key message across clearly and concisely. There are tools to help. One is called a message map.

In his Crystal Clear Communications blog post "What Is A Message Map?" George Stenitzer, who codeveloped this tool initially as a media interview technique for executives and spokespersons, points out that AT&T, The Home Depot, Intel, and the Chicago Metropolitan Agency for Planning (CMAP) all use message maps.

Here's why. Message Maps streamline thinking and drill down into the information required to support that thinking. This is illustrated in Figure 7.1.

You can dive more deeply into message maps and their use for a range of media, but it starts with the overarching idea you want to get across.

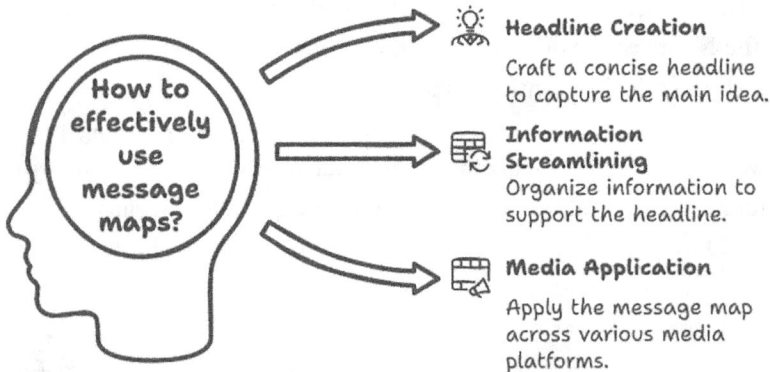

Headline Creation
Craft a concise headline to capture the main idea.

Information Streamlining
Organize information to support the headline.

Media Application
Apply the message map across various media platforms.

Figure 7.1 Using message maps effectively

Write this idea in the form of a headline at the top of the page and keep it simple. One sentence, at most, and a short sentence. Remember the old days of Twitter and 140 characters? Aim for that. Indeed, everything fits on one page.

Under the headline (aka the key message), note three positive points that support the headline. As Stenitzer notes in his blog, "Three is a magic number because it's the minimum number of points that enables humans to recognize patterns."

Under each point, there are story points to bring your message to life. These are examples, statistics, and anecdotes. The complete details don't need to be written down, rather use prompts that will remind you where you're going.

Let's try our hand at creating a message map for WartX.

Headline

WartX is a breakthrough treatment—safe, effective, innovative, and affordable.

Positive Point 1: Safe and effective
Story Points:

- WartX is a clinically tested treatment.
- It has FDA approval.
- Unlike traditional methods, WartX does not cause pain or scarring.

Positive Point 2: Innovative treatment
Story Points:

- Uses a proprietary ingredient that targets wart tissue without harming healthy skin.
- First-in-class nanotechnology. Micro-delivery particles penetrate the skin barrier and deliver treatment directly to the root of the wart ensuring complete removal.
- Highlights from the clinical trials: 30 percent faster clearance rates and a 20 percent lower recurrence rate.

Positive Point 3: It's about making people feel better—inside and out

Story Points:

- Not only removes warts but also strengthens the skin's barrier to prevent recurrence.
- Faster healing times and higher success rates compared to existing treatments like cryotherapy or salicylic acid.
- Simplifies treatment: easy-to-apply topical solution, no invasive procedures.

Whatever you have to say, you need to say it in a way that resonates with your audience. Like this (Figure 7.2):

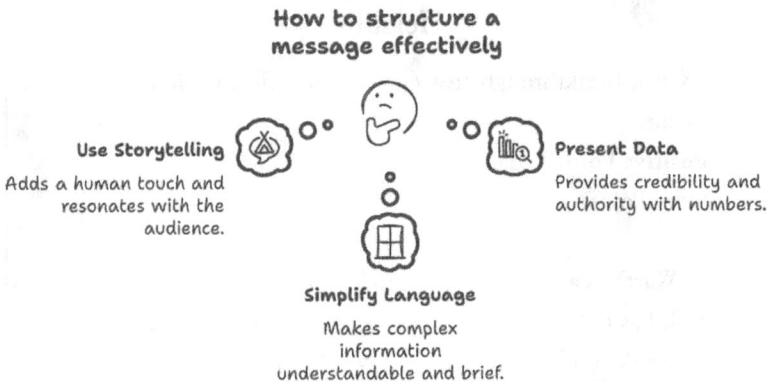

How to structure a message effectively

Use Storytelling
Adds a human touch and resonates with the audience.

Present Data
Provides credibility and authority with numbers.

Simplify Language
Makes complex information understandable and brief.

Figure 7.2 Structuring a message

A similar tool you may find useful is the message support stool shown in Figure 7.3.

One leg of the stool is intended for storytelling: anecdotes, case studies, real-life examples. These give your message a human face and resonate with audiences.

The second leg is data driven. It gives your message credibility and carries the voice of authority. It includes numbers, statistics, and figures. Not boring, heavy facts that overwhelm. It's about translating that data into meaningful information. For example, instead of saying "for $2,190 annually," you could say "for less than the cost of a cup of coffee a day."

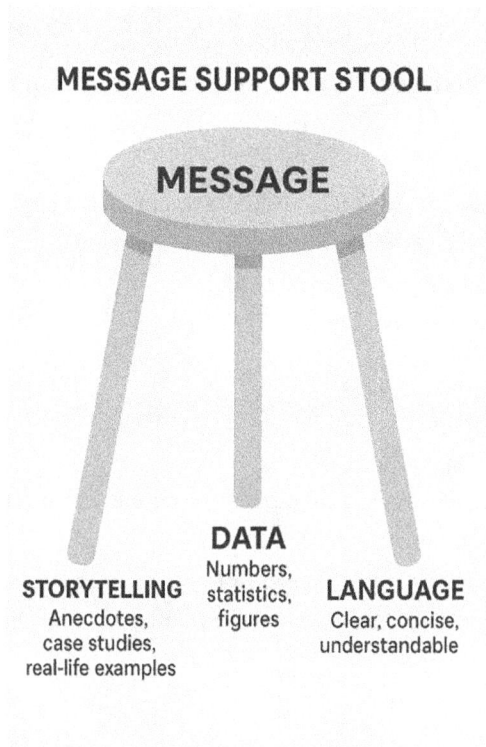

MESSAGE SUPPORT STOOL

MESSAGE

STORYTELLING
Anecdotes,
case studies,
real-life examples

DATA
Numbers,
statistics,
figures

LANGUAGE
Clear, concise,
understandable

Figure 7.3 Message support stool

The third leg: watch your language. This is about taking complex, qualified, expert, elevated information and making sure it is understandable—and brief. That might be a saying you use, a question you ask, a phrase you repeat. The subject isn't verruca vulgaris. We're talking warts.

Try this...

To prepare for an interview, identify three key messages. These are the headlines you'd like to see in the media. Under each message, list three stories you could tell, three stats you could offer up, and three understandable phrases or terms you could use. You'll be on topic, and interesting.

We took a stab at the exercise above. Here's what we came up with.

🔑 **Key Message 1:** WartX is a breakthrough in wart treatment.

Stories:

1. A look inside WartX's nanotechnology and how it targets wart roots.
2. A patient success story: a teen who had warts for years finally found relief—and a spot on *American Idol*.
3. Go behind the scenes of the FDA approval process—the process, the progress, and the pain.

Stats:

1. WartX demonstrated a **30 percent faster clearance rate** in clinical trials than other treatments.
2. Recurrence rates were **20 percent lower** than traditional treatments.
3. **FDA-approved** and clinically tested for both safety and efficacy.

Say what:

1. "This is next-gen wart removal."
2. "It goes straight to the root of the problem—literally."
3. "No more freezing, cutting, or waiting for a treatment to work. Maybe."

🔑 **Key Message 2:** WartX is safe, effective, and easy to use.

Stories:

1. How WartX helped a school nurse treat students quickly and discreetly.
2. Parents relief at finding a pain-free solution for their child's warts.
3. A pharmacist's take on why they recommend WartX.

Stats:

1. In user testing, **94 percent reported no pain** during treatment.
2. WartX caused no scarring in over 95 percent of cases.
3. Application time: less than **one minute a day**.

Say what:

1. "No pain, no problem."
2. "Gentle on skin, tough on warts."
3. "It's as easy as brush, cover, done."

🔑 **Key Message 3:** Warts are more than skin deep—and so is the solution.

Stories:

1. A young dancer finally performing barefoot again.
2. A teacher gaining confidence after clearing facial warts.
3. A clinic's move to offer WartX to underserved populations.

Stats:

1. **1 in 10 people worldwide** have warts—and many feel ashamed.
2. Among school-aged kids, prevalence is as high as **20 percent**.
3. WartX boosted self-reported confidence by **60 percent** post-treatment.

Say what:

1. "It's not just about skin. It's about confidence."
2. "Warts don't have to be part of your story."
3. "Helping people feel better—inside and out."

When the Going Gets Tough

Reporters will ask you all kinds of questions—for background, for details, for a clearer understanding, for human interest. Every once in a while, they'll ask you a question you'd rather not answer, or they'll ask it in a way that reframes the interview. There are numerous ways to deal with this. The first is to be prepared. The tools and techniques we just discussed will help you with this.

Another helpful technique to keep in mind if things don't go as planned: pivot. You don't always have to take the bait or rise to the challenge. Often used when the tenor of an interview is tense, pivoting enables you to remain on neutral ground—and your ground.

You're asked an inappropriate question—Why should we worry about warts when there are so many serious diseases? Aren't warts linked to uncleanliness? Why do witches have warts?—and you need to respond. The key is to make yourself and your organization look reasonable and approachable.

Pivoting lets you change the tenor of the question—and the course of the question. For instance:

Why should we worry about warts when there are so many serious diseases?

Great question. It's important to recognize that warts are rarely serious, but they are prevalent—and contagious. It's estimated roughly 10 percent of the population worldwide has warts, and this figure can hit 20 percent among school-aged children.

Aren't warts linked to uncleanliness?
Actually, warts are caused by the human papillomavirus (HPV). And they are contagious. That's why it's so easy to get warts in places like swimming pools where we are walking around barefoot, often with a cut or a scrape.

Why do witches have warts?
I'm going to turn that question over to Hermione Granger and her friends at the Hogwarts School of Witchcraft and Wizardry. But I will say, anyone who has a wart, witch or otherwise, WartX is here to help.

In some cases, questions can't be answered for a variety of reasons, often legal. The question may not apply to you, it may require information you can't divulge, or you may not have a definitive answer. It's helpful in these cases to explain why you can't answer the question. This explanation should make sense to viewers, sound reasonable, and give you an opportunity to get back to your key messages.

What did the FDA say about other wart treatments?

I can't speak for other companies—or the FDA. I can say WartX has FDA approval, and our clinical trials showed 30 percent faster clearance rates and a 20 percent lower recurrence rate.

How does WartX use nanotechnology?

That is proprietary information, as you can understand. What I can say is that, with WartX, micro-delivery particles penetrate the skin barrier and deliver treatment directly to the root of the wart ensuring complete removal.

I have a pimple. Can I use WartX?

WartX has never been tested for pimples. I'd suggest you ask your pharmacist. But if you have any warts, we can help.

Pivoting isn't about avoiding a question. It's about keeping the interview on track—and in a tone that is appropriate. Not answering a question is also risky. It may look like you're hiding something. That is also why answering "no comment," to a question is not a good idea. It's also why you need to be prepared for the questions you may not want to answer or that you feel are contentious. If you stutter or hesitate or look less than relaxed, this conveys discomfort at best, that you are hiding something at worst.

A tool to help you manage through an interview is to ask your media person/team to create a question and answer (Q&A) document that offers responses to all the questions that you anticipate good and bad.

When the Going Is Still Tough

Try these techniques to stick handle tricky questions.

- Get to the heart of the answer. "The real issue is…."
- Reframe the question initially. "What's important here…." Stick to your key message. If the reporter repeats the question, answer it.
- Give yourself some time to think. Ask the reporter to repeat the question or rephrase/summarize the question before answering. You can even say, "Sorry, I'm not sure what you mean."

- Point out the question isn't appropriate—nicely. "Good question, but unfortunately, it doesn't address the real issue." Or "I've heard this question before, and it assumes incorrectly that…."
- And, there is never anything wrong with saying, "I don't know." There is honesty and safety in acknowledging you don't have the expertise or the information at hand to answer a question. If the former, point the reporter to someone who does. If the latter, offer to get the information.

In her article in *PRNews*, "How To Field Hostile Questions During an Interview," Iris Dorbian offers the following tips:

- Reframe questions in neutral terms.
- Don't repeat hostile words or tone.
- Calmly ask to have vindictive questions repeated. This gives the questioner a chance to reconsider the rash statement and often succeeds in evoking moderation.
- Use a short pause. This will call attention to the question and may shift sympathy.
- Identify the real concerns behind the question. Knowing the person asking the question will help you respond more effectively.
- When sensory modes are used, reflect this in your response.
- If the questioner uses the sound mode, "Your plan sounds unrealistic," say, "I hear your concern; however, …."
- If the questioner uses a sight mode, "I don't see why you…," say, "Let me show you how the agency will…."
- If the questioner uses a touch mode, "I can't grasp why you…," say, "Let me touch on several issues…."
- If the questioner uses a feeling mode, "I have some strong feelings about the welfare of…," say, "We, too, are sensitive to the public interest and…."
- If the questioner doesn't use a particular mode, use a nonsensory response, such as "I understand," or use an affirmative gesture.

You can also have fun.

Toronto Maple Leafs Center Auston Matthews lost a tooth after slamming mouth first into a crossbar. After the game against the Pittsburgh

Penguins, a reporter asked him about the injury. "I saw the crossbar and I just decided that I think it would be a great idea if I just put my face right through it," Matthews said.

Building Bridges

Reporters, bloggers, and interviewers don't always ask questions in the way you'd like them asked. However, that doesn't mean you can't give the answer you want to give. Bridging is one technique that helps you do this. It enables you to get to the answer you want by building on the question you've been asked. This is usually done seamlessly and conversationally with a few opening words. The Alabama Department of Health uses a list of 33 bridging statements originally developed by Vincent T. Covello at the Center for Risk Communication in New York. Here are some of the items on the list:

> "And what's most important to know is…"
> "With this in mind, if we take a look back…"
> "If we take a broader perspective…"
> "What all this information tells me is…"
> "What this all boils down to is…"
> And as I said before…"
> And that reminds me…"

Bridging comes with caveats. It can make you look evasive and slick. What effective bridging does is let you get the interview back on track and highlight the key points relevant to the topic.

What bridging doesn't do—or shouldn't—is let you ignore tough questions. You should be prepared to answer these. This will make you look honest and helpful. Sometimes it's a matter of reframing the question.

Reporter: "Why are we spending money researching treatments for warts when there are so many serious diseases that need cures?"

Reframing the question: You raise an important point. Warts are not life-threatening but they are prevalent—and can affect how we see ourselves, especially among young people.

Keeping It Simple

Most interviews aren't confrontations. They're not a test of wills. They are questions asked, answers given. Both of these can be problematic. As a spokesperson or someone preparing a spokesperson, you can't change the questions that are asked, but you can make sure your answers are clear.

This is one of the biggest complaints reporters have: "expertise." It's a combination of legalese, bureaucratese, and computerese. It's often combined with psychobabble, gobbledygook, and technobabble. We live in worlds with abbreviations, acronyms, and technical terms that often don't have relevance beyond a select group of people. When we use this language to answer questions, you get confusion, boredom, frustration, and suspicion.

See for yourself. Joe Flood, in his article "Solar Storm: A Real-World Case for Plain Language" cites an article from *The Washington Post* that notes (1) an "X-class solar flare, the most intense type, is headed towards Earth," and (2) the National Oceanic and Atmospheric Administration (NOAA) and NASA don't agree on the severity; given this discrepancy, he wonders: *How would anyone know which prediction will turn out to be accurate?*

Here are two updates the organizations provided:

National Oceanic and Atmospheric Administration (NOAA)

> The latest model run now indicates the CME associated with yesterday's R3 (Strong) Radio Blackout event will impact the earth's magnetic field around 9:00 a.m. EDT (1300 UTC) on Saturday, July 14. SWPC is forecasting category G1 (Minor) Geomagnetic Storm activity then, with a chance of G2 (Moderate) levels at times through July 15. The S1 (Minor) Solar Radiation Storm persists just above event threshold. Region 1520 has decayed in the past 12 hours, but is still potentially eruptive.

National Aeronautics and Space Administration (NASA)

> Based on preliminary heliospheric modeling carried out at NASA GSFC Space Weather Center, it is estimated that the CME may impact Earth, Messenger, Spitzer, MSL, Mars. Simulations indicate that the leading edge of the CME will reach Earth at about 2012-07-14 T09:17Z (plus minus 7 hours). The roughly estimated expected range of the Kp maximum (Kp is a measure of geomagnetic disturbance levels ranging 0–9) is 6–8 (moderate to severe).

Ready for questions—check.

Getting Ready for an Interview: A Checklist

The following tips will get you prepared for even the toughest interviews, but keep in mind these are general tips. There may be more and other types of preparations necessary for some interviews.

Know your message. What do you want your audience to take away? Continue to emphasize these key themes throughout the interview.

Develop three or four key talking points that convey your message. Weave these points into your answers.

Anticipate what questions may be asked and be prepared with answers. If you are successful at staying on message, you can help shape the story.

Make sure your message is in plain language. Practice answers that sound conversational and will be instantly understood by the media outlet's audience.

Learn about the reporter and the outlet/site. Visit the outlet's website to read or watch their previous stories and find out more about their typical audience. The type of outlet will have an impact on the type of talking points that you prepare.

Learn about the story. Find out the goal of the story and try to get a sense of the types of questions that you may be asked.

Rehearse anticipated questions. After you get an idea of what the reporter might ask you, practice your answers to these questions a few

times. Even better, do it in front of a mirror, a friend, or a video camera. You can also do a mock interview with staff.

Relax and focus. Breathing exercises go a long way toward helping you relax and calm jittery vocal cords. Arrive at your interview
location, even if it's Zoom, 10 to 15 minutes early, and spend time
reviewing your core message points.

Chat with the interviewer. Right before the interview begins, chat
with the reporter to make sure you both have an understanding of the
topics that will be discussed. This is especially important for broadcast
interviews, so you do not get caught off guard on camera.

Before the interview, find out the following:

- What's the main thrust or angle of the interview?
- Who is the interviewer or news outlet? This will help you de-
  termine how to phrase your questions and answers.
- Does this interviewer have a previous position on the topic
  being discussed?
- What's their interview style?
- Who is the ultimate audience you're speaking to? Hint: It's not
  the reporter.
- Are there others being interviewed on this same topic?
- Can you anticipate their angle and its effect on your content?
  Can you preempt them?
- What is your primary theme for this interview?
- In one sentence, convey your main focus for the interview.
- What are the three major points that you want to make? Say-
  ing too much will dilute your message.
- What are the three most obvious or difficult questions you
  might be asked, or objections to your position, and your re-
  sponse to each?
- Do you have any appropriate anecdotes, analogies, or exam-
  ples to help reinforce and clarify your position?
- What visuals, if any, will help the interviewer and/or final audience more easily understand your message?

Final Reminders

Ask the interviewer in advance about the general subject matter to be covered and questions to expect.

- Why do you want to interview me?
- What are you hoping to get from the interview?

If you are not the appropriate person for the interview, inform the interviewer. You might suggest a more appropriate person in your organization.

Prepare your key messages and make sure you know them intimately. Remember: You can't control the media, nor can you control:

- The questions
- The direction of the interview
- Any biases held by the interviewer or the publication/outlet
- The headline or cutlines (the descriptive text that accompanies a photograph or video)
- The way you are portrayed
- The editing process (sometimes the interviewer has no control over editing either and may see the final story at the same time as you do)

But you CAN control what you say—and to do that you need to be prepared.

Decide what you should wear to project the image you want to convey about you and your organization. Clothes should be comfortable. Avoid jackets or suits with close-checked or herringbone patterns; the cameras cannot always cope with the intricacy of the pattern so viewers get an uncomfortable strobing effect. The same applies to closely striped shirts in sharply contrasting colors. Also avoid very dark suits, particularly in combination with white shirts, which can drain color from the face.

Relax. Go to the bathroom. Take a sip of water.

During an Interview: A Checklist

The following tips will help you during the toughest interviews.

Make your first words the most memorable. Interest levels diminish quickly, so make sure that the first words out of your mouth are on message and hit some of your key talking points.

Keep your audience in mind. The reporter you are speaking with is not your target audience. You are speaking to people as they watch the TV news in their living rooms, listen to the radio in their cars, or scroll news on the subway. Communicate in a way that engages them—speak like a real person; don't use jargon, technical terms, or acronyms, and always try to translate your "news" to their lives in a way that is relevant and compelling.

Be enthusiastic. Show your audience how interested you are in the topic. Now it is time to convey your compelling stories to readers, viewers, and listeners.

Keep your answers succinct. Don't feel compelled to keep talking. Most responses to questions should be 18 to 30 seconds. The average news clip is seven seconds.

Don't over-answer. When you feel the need to educate the reporter about everything that could be known about your project or issue, the interview loses focus. This also increases the chance of being misquoted. Keep answers short and to the point.

You shouldn't feel nervous when no one is talking. Wait for the reporter to ask you the next question.

Control the interview. You can steer the content of your interview. Remember your core message points and gently shift back to them in all of your answers.

If a reporter asks a question you cannot or won't answer, pivot or bridge the question. You might say, "I can't address that issue, but I can tell you…" (or) "That is interesting, but the issue here is…" If the reporter's question is vague, don't be afraid to ask for some clarification.

Localize and personalize. Try to make the topic personal to the audience. Including local facts or stories can make an interview more compelling to the listener as well as the reporter.

Never say "no comment." It makes you look guilty and untrustworthy. If you can't comment on a point, use a transitional phrase, such as "I'm not an expert on that subject, but…" and return to your message points.

Do not repeat negative words or inaccurate facts included in a reporter's question. Simply correct the inaccuracies and shift to an appropriate message point.

Don't worry about repeated questions. If the reporter's questions are the same, the content of your answers should remain the same. Reporters sometimes ask the same question more than once in order to get a simpler, cleaner answer. However, they may also be trying to get you to go further in your response than you may wish to.

Keep your eyes on the interviewer. If your eyes flicker around during a TV interview, you look uncomfortable, which can be misinterpreted. Keep your eye-line focused on the interviewer, then you come over as being in command of your subject. If you're really comfortable, look at the camera when you are making a key point.

Avoid frowning. With most topics, a smile won't be amiss at some point, especially the beginning or end of an interview.

At the end of the interview, reporters will often ask if there's anything else you'd like to tell them. Use this opportunity to drive your message home, even if you're repeating what you've already said. What should the audience take away from your interview? Repetition leads to more accurate reporting and better-informed audiences.

After an Interview: A Checklist

Review. Take some time to think about your questions and answers to prepare for your next interview.

Send follow-up information. This is a good opportunity to send the reporter any more information that you may have about the topics discussed in the interview. Keep good notes of any promise you made to follow up—and keep them.

Do a debrief. As a team, review interviews that are important, contentious, and/or typical. This will help you identify individual and collective areas for improvement.

Conduct an annual media audit. This will enable you to identify the type, nature, and extent of media coverage your organization gets and opportunities to enhance and extend coverage.

CHAPTER 8

Social Media Matters

The days are long gone when phrases like "online culture" and "it's gone viral" were either not used or meant something entirely different than they do today.

Entire generations have been raised with the ability to access information in real time at their fingertips. They've also been raised to understand that they don't just have a voice, they have many platforms through which they can express their views and experiences, both positive and negative. This has opened opportunities for expression that didn't exist prior to media moving from traditional to social, including extending your media efforts into spheres you might not otherwise find yourself.

This shifting environment is something large companies like Nike, Inc.; Sephora USA, Inc.; and Apple Inc. have all included as part of their media relations strategies. Influencer marketing, according to Statista, a global data platform, was forecasted to reach $39.33 billion by 2025.

For organizations without large budgets and huge numbers of employees, this new world can be daunting. However, using influencers doesn't have to mean finding those with a million followers and charging thousands for each post. It can also be about the right fit with someone who likes your product or believes in your services and what you represent.

If influencers are not the right fit for you, content creators may be. This is what real-life couple Rob and Sarah, who use Instagram as their main platform and go by the username tripseatravellers, call themselves. They travel the globe and have gained both a loyal following and the attention of businesses who thrive on tourism. According to Rob and Sarah, based on an interview,

an influencer is a person whose social media reflects their life and they would be hired and work with companies based on who they are, while content creators would be focused on photography and videography and showing places and experiences and would partner with companies based on the content they would create.

The pair suggest that hard-and-fast rules don't necessarily exist when it comes to establishing a budget for partnering with creators and influencers. Instead, it all depends on the organization and the type of partnership needed. But based on Rob and Sarah's experience, "the possibilities are endless."

This is the heart of social media.

While it has always been important for an organization to identify what it is and what it stands for, this is now more vital than ever. The onset of social media reinforced the need for businesses and organizations to deeply understand their own personalities, or brands.

That depth is necessary because we have more than one way of communicating who we are, and we can speak directly to and with an audience. And what we say has an echo. It may not come back to you right away, but it's out there. Someone else is hearing it and it's creating expectations. Therefore, knowing what you want to say is crucial because you have an opportunity to say it with more than words. Everything about your online presence speaks to who you are.

You can't build a relationship without expecting that the one you want to build a relationship with may want to get to know you better. Lindsay Schneider, founder of Get Into The Limelight, started her family-run business less than a decade ago. Since then she has grown her company from a Squarespace e-commerce store to a successful luxury line of sunless-tanning products and accessories stocked in stores across the United States and Canada.

According to Catherine Erdly in her article "Following This Simple Influencer Strategy Can Skyrocket Your Business," in *Forbes* (December 29, 2023), Schneider has been featured in well-known magazines and newspapers including *Cosmopolitan* and *The New York Times* and identifies long-term affiliate partnerships with influencers as pivotal to the success of her company by, in part, avoiding the costs of traditional advertising.

True North

Translating your organization into a personality is likely something you have already accomplished with a vision and mission statement.

If you have not done this, now is the time.

These documents are not just artifacts for your wall or an exercise to check off your list. They help identify the heart of your organization, who you want to be and, if there ever is a crisis to manage, how you will do so. They serve as your True North. Many businesses and organizations use strategic planning processes to gain insight into who they are resulting in vision, mission, and values statements. Such statements are vital for maintaining clarity in terms of direction and decision making. Equally vital is ensuring these statements are communicated with employees and are, as a result, integrated into your operations. These are important artifacts for any business to bring to life on all fronts, whether in an office, through a phone call, or online.

It's not just possible to translate all of this into posts for content sharing, into visuals used to promote messaging and define your online space, it's vital.

An easy and great example of this is Disneyland. As the professed, "Happiest Place on Earth," all content needs to reflect this theme. And it does. One look at their social pages shows you a world of smiles.

What it doesn't show you is constant sales pitches.

This is important to note because social media efforts should not be confused with an opportunity for a continual sales pitch. Social media platforms provide opportunities for users to learn from one another, to share insights and expertise, to highlight news and events, and to demonstrate your value to audiences without saying it in words.

Quality content makes the most of these opportunities. If you are constantly talking all about your goods and services, you risk losing the audience base you have spent time building. In fact, many social media leads swear by a rule of percentages. Percentages vary, but there is agreement that the lower number should be reserved for hard sales and a direct push for revenue.

One of the most popular breakdowns marketers use is 50/30/20 with the 50 percent representing interesting content that showcases who you are and engages an audience. Tips, fun facts, things that make people think or laugh. The 30 percent represents content that may originate from others but that aligns with the philosophy you hold. The final 20 percent is for promoting your business, services, or offers. This is not a hard-and-fast rule, and its origin is unknown despite its widespread use.

Content Distribution Strategy

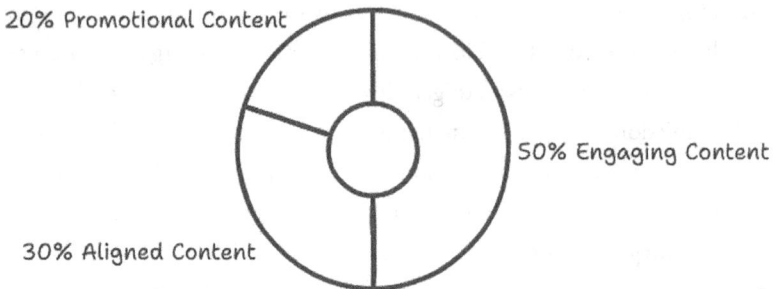

Figure 8.1 Content distribution strategy

Its purpose is to help provide a framework, as illustrated in Figure 8.1, for the type of posts you share.

How you should share is another story.

Increasingly, platforms that had been primarily text changed direction and allowed for video. In Above & Beyond: 2020 Sprout Social Index Deep Dive, video is still king. It's also cited as one of the best ways to connect with an audience and reach new followers. In this index, over 4,000 consumers, 900 social practitioners, and 300 marketing leaders across the United States, the UK, Canada, and Australia were surveyed. However, regardless of format, the content has to be interesting. It has to enable audience engagement and that means consistency.

For an audience to stay with you, they have to hear from you more than sporadically. You need to be a consistent presence and remind them that their perspective is valued. Enable feedback. Yes, this can get dicey. However, enabling feedback doesn't mean offering blanket opportunities for comments. You can state on your platforms what you represent and what will and can't be tolerated. Tell people what to expect. If you have booked a trip recently, you have likely been online looking at places to stay and taken a look at the reviews. Organizations can learn from such comments. It's important to respond to them in a way that lets people know you are serious. Audiences want authenticity, the root of which is this: If you say it, prove it. In other words, if you say you value customers, your customers should get that message without your having to use those words.

An effective social media strategy is aligned with your vision and reinforces your products, services, and values. It allows you to engage directly with your audience. The platforms you use need to work for you at a given point in time regardless of what's working for your competitor or another organization.

Strategies for Amplifying Media Coverage

Social media is also a great way to amplify media coverage. Use opportunities to augment messaging and ensure access to a broader audience. For example, livestream events and showcase a day in the life of an employee. Make yourself easy to find by placing QR code links to your website or platforms; use share buttons on media pitches and all news stories.

Understand Your Audience

You can't know what's being said about you—good or bad—if you are not part of the conversation. Since the onset of social media, listening has not only become much more important but also much easier.

Some organizations we have worked with have created a Twitter account, visited Facebook pages, blogs, and LinkedIn pages just to learn more about their competitors, hear what's being communicated, and to remain current about news related to their sector. Others use social media as a way of engaging their stakeholders in a dialogue about improving products and services. Starbucks Corporation, for example, launched a website called MyStarbucksIdea.com in 2008 encouraging visitors to submit suggestions on everything from coffee flavors to payment processes. Suggestions made by visitors to the site, who were no doubt customers, were reviewed and responded to on a blog providing updates regarding the status of the suggestions received.

Social media has impacted interests, changed expectations, and increased demands. Organizations must pay attention to concerns and questions and be ready with a response. To attract and retain an audience, organizations must also offer content that is interesting, visual, and that is in line with who they say they are.

On the flip side, organizations can now advertise globally with the click of a button. They can communicate directly with audiences and respond in real time. And social media can help act as a north star for your media relations. It can help you track coverage, reach, and engagement. It can help you assess your impact across platforms, channels, and outlets.

Social media amplifies your message, making it stronger and more impactful. Content published via news releases, e-mails, and other more traditional means can live longer, spread faster, and reach farther with the help of social media.

You can have a significant following, but without a social media strategy to incorporate into your brand strategy and to sustain your online messaging, you run the risk of falling flat. A well-developed social media strategy can support a business, organization, and/or an individual in communicating more broadly, in reinforcing a brand, and in generating increased interest in products, services, and events.

CHAPTER 9

Pitch Perfect

"Please think about the journalist you are reaching. S/he is reading 100 PR pitches a day. All of them are bad. Not most. Not almost all. All of them. That is the overwhelming rule of PR pitches. They are all bad. Because they are not useful."

—Derek Thompson, Staff Writer, *The Atlantic*

Crafting News Releases, Backgrounders, and More

Traditionally, organizations primarily reached out to media with a news release. Tradition is changing, thanks in large part to social media and the downsizing of news outlets. Still, the release has a role to play today—an important role. Wire services, which distribute releases, can have more than 200,000 outlets and 10,000 websites on their list. That's a big reach. The question, of course, is how relevant are those outlets to the message you want to share?

Therein lies the success of the media release, indeed, of any pitch. Therein lies what annoys *The Atlantic's* Derek Thompson so much. Quantity does not replace quality.

Before we delve into what makes a good release, let's look at what constitutes a news release. This has not changed significantly over the years. The release takes the form of an inverted pyramid as in Figure 9.1.

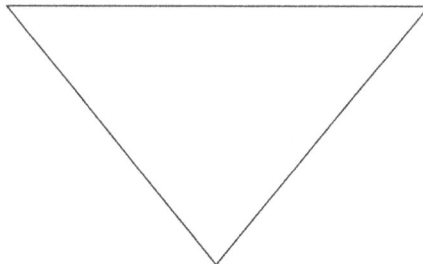

Figure 9.1 Inverted pyramid

Most of the questions reporters, producers, bloggers, and others need answered can be found up front at the widest part of the pyramid: who, what, where, when, why, and how. Supporting details and quotes flesh out the remainder of the release. Contact information, for images and interviews, usually comes at the end, although, as in the example below, it can come at the beginning.

A template for a news release looks like this one from Smartsheet Inc.

STANDARD PRESS RELEASE

CONTACT INFORMATION:

    [Company Name]

    [Contact Name]

    [Phone Number]

    [E-mail Address]

YOUR LOGO

RELEASE DATE:

    [Date]

    [MAIN PRESS RELEASE HEADLINE {*ALL CAPS*}]

    [Optional Subhead {*Title Case/*Italicized**}]

    Dateline: [CITY, STATE, Month Date]—Lede: [Briefly and explicitly state the information you need to share. Include who, what, when, where, why, and how and lead with the most important information.]

    Body paragraphs: [Background information, rich quotes, etc.]

    [Boilerplate]

    [Call to Action]

    ###

The first press release is said to have been issued in 1906 in the wake of a train disaster in New Jersey that killed 50 people. Ivy Ledbetter Lee, the Pennsylvania Railroad Company's PR person, issued a release to get ahead of the onslaught of calls from reporters. What he got was pushback. Reporters and editors declared this was an attempt at free advertising.

In response, Lee wrote and distributed what he called his Declaration of Principles. They are still valid today. Here's some of what Lee had to say:

> "This is not a secret press bureau. All our work is done in the open. We aim to supply news. This is not an advertising agency; if you think any of our matter ought properly to go to your business office, do not use it. Our matter is accurate. Further details on any subject treated will be supplied promptly, and any editor will be assisted most cheerfully in verifying directly any statement of fact. Upon inquiry, full information will be given to any editor concerning those on whose behalf an article is sent out. In brief, our plan is, frankly and openly, on behalf of business concerns and public institutions, to supply to the press and public of the United States prompt and accurate information concerning subjects which it is of value and interest to the public to know about. Corporations and public institutions give out much information in which the news point is lost to view. Nevertheless, it is quite as important to the public to have this news as it is to the establishments themselves to give it currency. I send out only matter every detail of which I am willing to assist any editor in verifying for himself. I am always at your service for the purpose of enabling you to obtain more complete information concerning any of the subjects brought forward in my copy."

The intent of a news release is to alert reporters and others to reliable information that may be of interest to them. It is not the expectation that the release will be used verbatim although this is often the hope—and it was the case in 1906. *The New York Times* ran the release as written by Lee, although they acknowledged its source and did not imply this was a "story" written by a reporter.

If the intention of a release is to alert reporters et al to a possible story, then the natural expectation is that the organization will be available for further comment, interviews, and follow-up questions unless otherwise stated. Distributing a release is the first step—and it implies a commitment that you are willing to and available for interviews and follow-up.

Many organizations gripe about a lack of success using news releases. This may be, in part, a volume issue. Media receive many, many pitches; they can't use them all. And today there are fewer reporters and editors to review those releases.

There are many other reasons for a lack of response, including bad timing. For example, if you're a health nonprofit and the outlet has just run three stories featuring nonprofits in the health sector, or if the outlet quoted your organization in a recent story, they may be reluctant to use you again—especially if you are in the private sector.

Bottom line

The number one reason releases don't get picked up is because they are not newsworthy.

There has to be a reason why your story should run and should run now. It's right in the title of the tool: news release. Yes, your organization just turned four and that is a milestone—for your organization, not necessarily for the wider community or the nation. You're having your annual art auction to raise money for a worthy cause, but the art auction is not a new event and there are many charities raising money by hosting fundraising events. You have a new product, and you want the world to know. That's what advertising does. You want to raise awareness about homelessness in your community; you'll need more than the issue. You'll need a hook—a new report, a change in the status quo such as fewer shelters, or a twist on a familiar topic—meteorologists are predicting the coldest winter on record. What will this mean for people who have nowhere to sleep indoors?

It's also helpful to find the story in your story. Look at what you're pitching from the reporter or blogger's point of view. What stands out? What is different? What adds to the ongoing understanding?

We once wrote a news release for a local animal shelter that was hosting its annual Bowling for Critters fundraising event. The event wasn't new, the format of the evening was the same, the goal hadn't changed—and there are many worthy causes in the community, all looking for media attention.

Take a moment to see how you would write this release.

Now take a look to see what we did. The response was significant—and camera crews turned out for the event.

NEWS RELEASE

Bide Awhile Animal Shelter goes to the dogs—and the bowling alley

DATE | HALIFAX | The bowler looks relaxed. He assesses the angle, moves slowly forward on the lane, and lines up the shot. Then he releases the ball—with his nose. The bowler is one of the dogs who is showing off their prowess as part of the annual Bide Awhile Animal Shelter's Bowling for Critters, which will take place at the Fairlanes Bowling Centre, Halifax Shopping Centre, on Saturday, January 19, from 6:00 p.m. to 9:00 p.m.

"The bowling dogs have officially kicked off our event for many years. They do amazingly well. In fact, their scores are often higher than our two-legged bowlers," says [NAME], president of the board of directors, Bide Awhile Animal Shelter.

The annual Bowling for Critters event brings together more than 30 teams and 120 bowlers from across Nova Scotia to raise much-needed funds for the province's largest, independent animal shelter. "This year the money raised is earmarked for the building of our new shelter, which will enable us to ultimately provide a home for more dogs and cats in Halifax Regional Municipality," says [NAME].

Bide Awhile is currently turning away 30 animals a day. There are thousands of homeless cats in HRM but only an estimated 200 combined kennel spaces, and only two shelters. And Bide Awhile is the only shelter in HRM to routinely accept animals from owners giving up their pets. The new facility on Neptune Crescent in the Woodside Industrial Park, Dartmouth, will help to significantly address this situation.

"We are committed to increasing the number of animals we rescue by 100 per cent, but we cannot make this happen without improving our efficiency in an expanded building," says [NAME].

> Members of the public are welcome to drop by the Fairlanes Bowling Centre to watch the dogs and their two-legged friends hit a few pins, place a bid on silent auction items (including a fabulous, framed artwork from [XXX] Gallery that captures a contemplative cat), guess the number of dog and cat treats crammed into a bowl, and have a fabulous and furry time.

The success of media relations tools like news releases depends on your information getting into the right hands. There are two broad approaches to this: (1) toss a pebble into the ocean and hope it washes up where you wanted, or (2) drill down into who is likely to run with your story. The latter is more successful. It's also more work.

There's a four-step process for organizing information before writing (and distributing) that is discussed in donalee's book *The Thong Principle: Saying What You Mean and Meaning What You Say*. We're going to review it here and put the process in the context of media relations, specifically pitching.

The best approach to getting a message out into the world is to think first, then communicate. This is especially important if we don't know our audience well, if the subject is lengthy or complex, or if the issue is sensitive. This four-step process helps identify what information should be included, how to organize that information, and the appropriate tone. The components are:

- Purpose
- Audiences
- Key messages
- Proof

Purpose

It sounds like such a simple thing: Why am I writing? Too often, though, we are unclear about our purpose or our purpose is too broad to be attainable. To ensure we create the content needed to achieve our purpose, we need to be able to state that purpose in one simple sentence.

For example, we might say: The purpose of this news release is to make WartX the best-selling wart treatment on the market.

On the surface, we have accomplished the first step in the process. It's one sentence, and it contains a goal. And it will not work. The goal is too broad; it is not the role of reporters to wave our flag; and one news release is not going to propel our company to the top of the New York Stock Exchange.

Let's try this. The purpose of this news release is to highlight data from a new report released by the National Association for Mental Health that shows a growing connection between body image and depression among young women in America.

Very specific. More realistic. You'll also notice the purpose isn't about touting the benefits of WartX. It's about positioning RenewSkin Sciences as knowledgeable and up to date about issues related to its products. In all likelihood, others will also be interviewed for a story on this topic. We may even want to partner with an organization and jointly issue the release. We will, if possible, want to include a quote from a dermatologist and/or patient that adds a human face to the data in the new report.

Audiences

Again, this sounds simple. Our audience is the media. Or influencers, bloggers. Too often we know who we're communicating with in a broad sense, but we haven't really thought about their needs. This step helps us do that.

There are two key aspects of our audience that we are interested in. First, what do we know about them? What is our relationship? The answers will affect both content and tone. Usually the better we know someone, the friendlier we can sound. We can be more informal, more conversational and casual. This will be particularly important for one-on-one pitches directed to specific individuals.

The second thing we want to know about our audience is their level of knowledge about the subject. The more they know, the less information we have to provide. The less they know, the more description, explanation, and examples will be needed. The more they know, the more we can use technical terms, jargon, and acronyms. The less they know, the plainer and more straightforward our language needs to be.

If we think about the release highlighting the new report from the National Association for Mental Health, we know we're most likely pitching to health reporters or media outlets, youth-related bloggers, perhaps specialized audiences like dermatologists. This is not the same people to whom we'd issue a release at Halloween talking about the history of warts.

Now we know why we're communicating and with whom. It's time to figure out what to say.

Key Messages

We know a lot of details about the subject we're communicating. Our audience rarely needs—and certainly doesn't want—all those details. We have to narrow down what's necessary for them to know and what can safely be omitted. Key messages help us do just that.

Key messages are broad, general statements that summarize the main points of our communication. They're linked to our purpose. And they are few in number. We can't have 24 key messages. We'll leave our readers and our listeners in a fog.

We need to zero in on what is most important. If our audience remembers only one or two things after reading our message, what do we want them to remember? Those are our key messages.

Let's put this in the context of our release. Our key messages might be:

- Twenty-six percent of American girls say they are depressed because of how they look—and the number one cause of distress is blemishes.
- According to the National Association for Mental Health report, young women are trying unsafe treatments to improve their body image.

Proof

This is about concrete language. This is about offering data, statistics, facts, examples, testimonials, and more that bring our key messages to life and imbue them with credibility. We don't say something is important, we show that it is. We don't suggest something is a good idea, we demonstrate it is. In doing so, we build our credibility. This builds interest in our story.

In the case of the body image story, we have an entire report to draw on. We also have our own experts we can quote, and we may have patients or parents who would like to speak up on this issue.

Pitch Perfect

The news release is usually a broad outreach to numerous reporters and writers. More and more often today, we're reaching out to one reporter or writer with a pitch. This is the equivalent of the elevator pitch where you have 30 seconds to convince an investor your ideas warrant their hard-earned money. Because pitches tend to be targeted to one media outlet or one type of reporter, doing your homework is essential. It starts with finding out what the publication wants and needs. What types of stories do they run and, equally important, what stories don't they run.

In that same vein, try to mirror the style and tone of the outlet, the blogger, the influencer. Spend some time reading and listening to what they've published. Be a Scout, be prepared.

And be original. Nothing annoys reporters more than being pitched an idea for a story they've already run—or their competition has run. If your idea has a twist, spell this out early in the pitch.

A typical pitch often follows this format:

- Short, clear subject line that draws the reader in
- An introduction to you and your reason for writing. Make this as relevant to the reader as possible, e.g., I'm following up on your recent blog about warts and frogs. It had me scratching my head.
- A reason why readers would be interested
- Contact info

Here's an example JustReachOut, a PR support firm, posted on their site.

Hi Jessica.

I just read your story on the health benefits of the keto diet.

I've got a good one for you: a new survey of 2,000 keto followers found 87% of keto dieters report that they cheat on the diet.

Happy to provide more context and findings.

Thanks.

Brian

CHAPTER 10

The Media Audit

Having a media relations plan is important. Making sure that plan is working is equally important. Evaluation is central to most every program and initiative your organization will undertake. Media relations is no exception.

As with many of the evaluations an organization conducts, there are qualitative and quantitative options. In the context of media relations, the former might include focus groups, comments from reporters, anecdotal feedback, and social media posts. The latter might encompass surveys, data analytics from social media and websites, and year-over-year comparisons. And, of course, there are the goals (the measurable goals) spelled out in the media plan itself. Were these met? Why or why not?

In addition to standard evaluation options, there is a tool unique to media relations. The media audit. A media audit for earned media (as opposed to advertising) is a strategic review of an organization's media coverage across various platforms—print, digital, broadcast, and social media. Its primary purpose is to evaluate how the organization, its messaging, leadership, and products or services are represented in the media.

Historically, media audits were conducted manually, often relying on clipping services and some poor employee hunched over mounds of paper taking notes and recording a variety of statistics. In the past, these audits served primarily as retrospective tools—used to measure the impact of media initiatives or to justify budgets. However, the rise of digital media, social platforms, and real-time analytics has transformed the audit into a more dynamic, continuous process.

Today's media audits are more comprehensive and data driven. They incorporate social listening tools, sentiment analysis, audience engagement metrics, and cross-platform comparisons. They are no longer limited to traditional news media but also include blogs, influencer content, podcasts, and online reviews. With increased attention to misinformation, brand reputation, and media polarization, audits now also play a critical role in risk management and strategic planning.

Recent trends show a growing emphasis on qualitative analysis, not just counting mentions or impressions. Organizations want to know *how* they're being talked about, *who* is shaping the narrative, and *what* messages are resonating. There's also a stronger focus on diversity, equity, and inclusion in media representation as well as regional versus national visibility, and alignment with organizational values.

Ultimately, a well-executed media audit helps organizations move beyond visibility to influence—helping to shape the conversation rather than just being a sound bite.

The Way Things Were

Let's take a look at the seven major components of a traditional media audit. Many of these elements are still relevant today.

Length

The length of the media item—measured in word count, duration (for broadcast), or column inches—can indicate the importance or depth of coverage. Longer pieces may reflect greater editorial interest or complexity of the subject. It's about substance.

For example: A *Globe and Mail* feature on WartX's development lab ran over 1,200 words, and a Q101 radio clip made reference to WartX as part of a 36-second intro to a Hallowe'en contest. It's logical to conclude the former reflects in-depth coverage and sustained reader engagement. The latter is fun and fleeting.

Placement

This refers to where a piece appears. In print, this might be the front page, business section, or a home page feature. Online it might be the opening, middle, or bottom of a blog. For broadcast, it signals the top of the newscast, the midpoint, or the end. Prominent placement usually equates to higher visibility and perceived importance.

For example: An article about WartX's latest product was featured on the home page of CBC News for 12 hours, suggesting strong editorial interest and relevance. Compare this to a blog post that contains only a link to the product in the last paragraph.

Visuals

Visual elements include photos, graphics, infographics, charts, and videos that may accompany the coverage. These enhance storytelling and can influence how engaging or shareable the content is. Visuals often draw readers and listeners in and can help to keep them engaged.

For example: The CBC News segment included a behind-the-scenes look at WartX's Halifax office and drone footage of their facility. Then there was the blog—no visuals.

Quotes

Quotes from company spokespeople, partners, customers, or experts can shape perception and build credibility. Strong, well-positioned quotes reinforce messaging. They also give a human face to your organization. From a messaging perspective, this helps to appeal to the emotional response of audiences. No quotes may indicate a lesser role in the story.

For example: WartX CEO Jana Boudreau was quoted in the *Globe* as saying, "We're not just helping teenagers get rid of warts—we're helping them feel better about themselves." This reinforces the company's strategic messaging on mental health and body image.

Theme

Stories are about something. There is a focus, or angle as reporters often call it. This is the underlying narrative of the piece. It could be innovation, controversy, success, or human interest. As part of the media audit, you'll want to identify the theme and if it aligns with your values and messaging.

For example: Most recent coverage of WartX revolved around the theme of tech leadership, positioning the company as a national health care innovator rather than a regional player. This is positive positioning, but you may decide to reinforce the treatment success, and not tech advances, in future media plans.

Tone

Stories convey more than facts. They have a tone, broadly described as positive, negative, or neutral (and in some cases a combination of those). A long, in-depth article with a negative tone may be more damaging than helpful. You need to be rigorous here. It helps to have more than one person assess tone, so you don't hear what you want to hear.

For example: Coverage of WartX's mental health-awareness efforts with teens is very positive, with the *Toronto Star* describing the company's work as "a model for other healthcare companies."

Outlet

This refers to the publication or platform where a piece appears. Consider reach, audience demographics, political or industry alignment, and editorial standards.

For example: WartX was recently mentioned in an article about skin care in *Cosmopolitan*. It was only a mention, but the publication has a significant reach. There are 64 international editions in over 35 languages in 110 countries getting into the hands of more than 100 million people. The monthly magazine has a combined print and digital circulation of 405,308 and readership is approximately five times that number.

The Way Things Are Now

While the foundational elements of a traditional audit still matter, today's media landscape demands a broader, faster, and more nuanced approach (Figure 10.1). Let's revisit WartX—through the lens of a contemporary media audit. Think of this as an evolution from clipboard to dashboard.

Media Audit Framework

(with WartX examples)

Sentiment Analysis & Social Listening

Detect tone, trends, and emotional nuance across platforms

72% positive sentiment spike after ‚Skin Smart' app launch

Engagement Metrics

Measures depth of audience interaction, not just reach

1 2M YouTube views but low average watch time → Shorter videos created

Influencer & Micro-Influencer Impact

Tracks collaboration success and audience trust

@dermwithdev boosted page traffic by 26%, Micro-In-fluencers performed best

Message Penetration & Consistency

Evaluates alignment and repetition of core messages

‚Safe and easy' message hit 68% of coverage 'Breakthrough underper-formed at 28%

Diversity & Representation Analysis

Looks at whose voices are amplified and whose aren't

Competitive Benchmarking

Compares your visibility, sentiment, and strategy to key rivals

Real-Time & Ongoing Monitoring

Allows for timely adjustments and continuous improvement

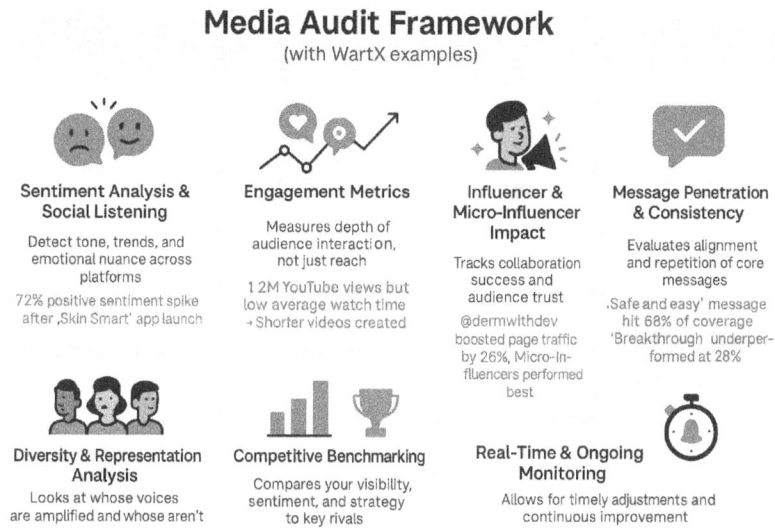

Figure 10.1 Media audit framework

Sentiment Analysis and Social Listening

Automated tools like Meltwater, Brandwatch, or Talkwalker can scan thousands of posts, articles, and comments to detect tone, trends, and traction. Instead of simply classifying content as "positive" or "negative," they detect emotional nuance and map sentiment over time.

For example: Over a three-month period, sentiment analysis of WartX-related content on Twitter/X, Reddit, and TikTok revealed a 72 percent positive perception among teens and young adults, with spikes following a viral post about the company's new "Skin Smart" app. A dip occurred during a brief controversy over user data, which was quickly resolved—also traceable through social listening.

Engagement Metrics

The emphasis here is on engagement: comments, shares, likes, click-throughs, time spent on page. This reflects actual audience interaction with the message and goes beyond reach or impressions.

For example: A YouTube video about WartX's wart-detection tool garnered 1.2 million views. On the surface, this is fabulous. But we need to dig beneath the surface. An audit showed that the average view duration was only 28 seconds of a two-minute video. This prompted the communications team to develop shorter, more dynamic content.

Influencer and Micro-Influencer Impact

Influencer content assesses the reach and relevance of influencer collaborations.

For example: A partnership with Halifax-based skincare influencer @dermwithdev resulted in a 26 percent traffic increase to WartX's acne-treatment page. Interestingly, micro-influencers (under 50K followers) showed higher engagement and conversion rates than celebrities.

Message Penetration and Consistency

Key messages need to resonate—and this part of the audit helps us to understand how our messages were received and if they were repeated. AI tools can scan large volumes of content to determine message alignment.

For example: WartX's media plan includes three messages: (1) WartX is a safe, effective, and easy solution for wart removal. (2) WartX is a breakthrough in wart treatment. (3) Living with warts is not painless. Removing them can be. The audit showed message the first message appeared in 68 percent of coverage, the third in 55 percent. Message #2 was reflected in only 23 percent of coverage—indicating a need to reinforce this moving forward or rethink the message itself.

Diversity and Representation Analysis

It's important to understand how different communities are represented in both content and coverage.

For example: WartX's audit included a demographic breakdown of voices quoted in articles and featured in media content. It revealed that while the company's leadership (primarily women) was well represented, racial and geographic diversity was lacking in quoted health care professionals and patient testimonials.

Competitive Benchmarking

Today's audits don't exist in a vacuum. Many organizations benchmark against competitors to identify gaps and opportunities.

For example: WartX's audit compared its media visibility and sentiment to two national competitors. WartX ranked higher in engagement but lower in mentions on medical-news platforms. The insight prompted the PR team to target health care–specific media more deliberately.

Real-Time and Ongoing Monitoring

Contemporary audits are less about a once-a-year check-in and more about continuous improvement. Dashboards deliver real-time insights that allow for adjustments as the media plan unfolds.

For example: During a national rollout of WartX's new acne product, real-time media monitoring identified confusion around application instructions. The comms team responded by releasing an explainer video and briefing partner pharmacists—improving customer satisfaction and reducing comments and calls.

Modern media audits do more than look backward; they inform strategy moving forward. A well-executed audit today is not just a mirror but a compass—pointing the way to smarter, more resonant media relations.

CHAPTER 11

Back to the Future

"The future ain't what it used to be."

—Yogi Berra, Baseball Catcher, Manager, and Coach

Media relations has been and will continue to be about putting yourself out there, openly, honestly, and strategically. What you share and how you share it is ultimately determined by you and for your organization's benefit. Your media outreach also needs to consider the group on the other end of your information sharing, the media. What do they need, how do they need it, and how can your relationship coexist in a way that enables both of you to get what you need and want.

These questions underpin the nature of media relations. They will continue to be its foundation. The answers, on the other hand, will evolve. While we can't know with certainty what's coming, we can make a few predictions.

On the Horizon

Welcome to AI World—And More

AI is redefining the media and, as a result, media relations. There are AI news casts, AI anchors, AI-generated stories. The technology that creates avatars to deliver the news isn't just emerging. It's old news.

In January 2024, BBC Features Correspondent Chris Stokel-Walker wrote an article detailing how a Los Angeles based start-up planned to start showing AI-generated news. In "TV channels are using AI-generated presenters to read the news. The question is, will we trust them?" Stokel-Walker noted that the start-up, known as Channel 1, was "the latest demonstration of AI-powered news presenters around the world." A segment in Greece had already run in May 2023. South Korea, India, and Taiwan were either using or exploring AI-generated news.

Communications professionals are also using AI to quickly and effectively create content and engage audiences—including reporters, bloggers, influencers, and others. Thanks to AI much of that content, positioning, and outreach can now be personalized to meet specific interests and needs. The use of this technology makes translation between languages easier, reduces reliance on detailed Internet searching, and enables processing information faster than any human brain.

AI will also continue to become central in evaluation. It can analyze huge amounts of data to offer real-time public sentiment analysis, leading to more effective and focused initiatives.

Evolving along with AI is the media landscape itself. New platforms and new tech will undoubtedly emerge. Niche streaming platforms like Nebula (for educational creators) and Shudder (for horror fans) are already gaining traction, while immersive media experiences—such as virtual reality documentaries on Meta Quest or augmented reality (AR) news overlays from apps like *The New York Times'* AR features—will play a growing role in media consumption. For media relations, these represent a brave new world with inherent opportunities and pitfalls. Organizations may need to tailor press releases for virtual press rooms, create pitch materials optimized for voice-activated assistants, or even craft stories that can be told interactively through virtual reality (VR) environments.

Not surprisingly social media will continue to be a dominant force in communication. Traditional press releases will take even more of a backseat as organizations turn to social platforms to make announcements and connect with audiences in real time. This will mean the need to keep an eye out for the new and emerging platforms and to understand which demographics are drawn to which option.

This direct-to-consumer communication eliminates the need for journalists as gatekeepers in some cases, but it will remain imperative to see how media can be included in any organizational outreach. Reporters, bloggers, and others will remain as key audiences.

Moving forward, influencer partnerships will play a greater role in online dissemination of credible information. Depending on the level of trust they create with their audiences, their opinions and preferences will carry even more weight. As a result, the next iteration of their involvement in your media relations plan will be longer-term, authentic relationships.

Organizations will continue to tell their own stories—and share those stories with reporters in the broadest sense of the word. Technology will enable multimedia storytelling that is relatable and affordable. An increasing appetite for dimensional stories will fuel their creation. Dimensional stories go beyond simply telling a narrative; they incorporate multiple dimensions to create a richer and more impactful experience for the audience. This involves considering various aspects of the story, including its emotional depth, the context it's presented in, and how it connects with the audience on a deeper level.

On the Flip Side of AI

At the same time AI makes it easier to develop and distribute information—through tools like automated press release generators, chatbots for media inquiries, or AI-assisted content creation—there is a strong and growing call for authenticity and transparency. These are values that cannot simply be espoused; they must be lived. For example, companies that use AI-generated statements without disclosing them risk losing public trust, as seen in the recent backlash against undisclosed synthetic content in political campaigns and corporate messaging. On the other hand, organizations that openly communicate their use of AI, such as *The Washington Post*'s clear labeling of AI-assisted reporting, are often praised for their honesty. Organizations will be held accountable for what they say and how they say it. Both these critical attributes—authenticity and transparency—are not just ethical expectations, they are strategic imperatives built into a sound media relations plan.

They are also linked to employee engagement. Employees are credible voices—and powerful ones. For example, when Microsoft employees publicly supported the company's stance on ethical AI use, it strengthened the company's media messaging by showing internal alignment and authenticity. Similarly, hospital staff sharing real stories on social media during the COVID-19 pandemic provided powerful, trusted insights that often received media pickup. Employees can become inherent elements of a media relations plan—serving as spokespeople, storytellers, or subject-matter experts—ensuring, of course, that their involvement is voluntary, transparent, and aligned with the organization's values.

Media relations 2.0 will not be solely focused on technology to transmit and transform messages. The human connection will remain vitally important. Sustained relationships with reporters, bloggers, and influencers will be crucial as they are today. The need to understand media outlets' perspectives, style, and audience demands will not diminish. Indeed, in an increasingly fragmented world, this may become more important. Pitches will remain a central component of media relations—and, at their best, these are always targeted.

Where we are today is not where we will be tomorrow or the day after tomorrow. Successfully embracing the path ahead means looking back from where we have come and taking what we've learned on the new journey ahead.

No matter what that journey holds, an organization's relationship with the media will be paramount.

Appendixes

Appendix A

Guidelines on the Provision of Information to the News Media
   U.S. Department of Health & Human Services
   Office of the Assistant Secretary for Public Affairs
   January 2022

Background

The Department of Health and Human Services (HHS) is the United States government's principal agency for protecting the health of all Americans and providing essential human services. HHS and its family of agencies manage more than 300 programs encompassing scientific research, public health services, food and drug safety, health care services, health insurance, and a host of child support and enrichment programs.

HHS is committed to a culture of openness with the media and public that values the free exchange of ideas, data, and information and doing so in a manner that is timely, responsive, and accurate. To honor this commitment, HHS expects its employees to abide by the following set of core communications principles:

- Be honest and accurate in all communications
- Honor publication embargoes
- Respond promptly to media requests and respect media deadlines
- Act promptly to correct the record or erroneous information, when appropriate
- Promote the free flow of scientific and technical information
- Promote plain writing of media documents and releases
- Create greatest transparency possible through distributing information timely and widely through internet, email, media wires, and other mechanisms
- Protect confidential, classified, and non-public information

Purpose and Scope

This document provides guidance on the provision of information to news media. This is defined as information in any form provided to news and information media, especially information that has the potential to generate media attention, public interest, or inquiry.

Examples include, *but are not limited to*, interviews, press releases, media advisories, editorial boards, letters to the editor, opinion-editorial columns, audio or video news releases, B-roll (video footage provided free of charge to broadcast news organizations), and blogs and other Internet postings used to convey news or items of public interest. *Not* included under this definition are scientific and technical reports or articles and technical information in professional journals.

These guidelines are applicable to all Operating Divisions (OPDIV), Staff Divisions (STAFFDIV), Offices, and other programs (henceforth referred to as "agency") within the Department of Health and Human Services, as well as all HHS employees, fellows, and other non-full-time employees employed by HHS. In the event of any conflict between this guidance and any other HHS policy, directive, or regulation, this guidance shall govern and supersede any previous issuance or directive.

Responsibilities

Office of the Assistant Secretary for Public Affairs

The HHS Office of the Assistant Secretary for Public Affairs (ASPA) is the principal point of contact, at the national level, for news media and general public inquiries about the Department of Health and Human Services and its agencies.

ASPA is responsible for:

- Conducting and coordinating news media relations for the department
- Establishing news media, including online news media, relations policies and priorities
- Coordinating and reviewing the performance of all news media relations activities
- Coordinating these activities with HHS leadership, and OPDIVs and STAFFDIVs
- Clearing news media releases, activities, events, and materials
- Ensuring timely release and efficient dissemination of materials and information to news media
- Editing to ensure that public information products are written in plain language, consistent with Associated Press style, and in line with news media principles, practices, and expectations, while maintaining the integrity of the scientific or technical data and the meaning of programmatic content.

Directors of OPDIVs, STAFFDIVs, Offices and Programs

Operating Division (OPDIV), Staff Division (STAFFDIV), office and program directors have ultimate responsibility for the technical, scientific, and programmatic accuracy of all information that is related to their respective programs and released by HHS.

OPDIV, STAFFDIV, Office and Program Communications/Public Affairs/Media Relations Officers

These individuals must notify ASPA in a timely manner about activities or events that have the potential to generate media or public interest or inquiry.

All HHS Employees and Programs

All HHS employees and programs are required to coordinate, in a timely manner, with the appropriate agency media relations office prior to releasing information that has the potential to generate media or public interest.

Guidelines

General Guidelines

HHS seeks to provide the widest practical and appropriate dissemination of information concerning its activities, programs, and recommendations. News media and journalist requests, including blogger requests, for public information concerning HHS activities and the results of HHS activities should be addressed promptly, factually, and as completely as possible, in accordance with applicable federal laws and regulations.

To ensure timely responses for requests for information, HHS will strive to ensure cooperation and coordination among the agency's scientific and public affairs communities. HHS agencies and offices will comply with directives, procedures, and guidance from ASPA at HHS.

In keeping with the desire for a culture of openness, HHS employees may, consistent with this policy, speak to members of the press about their work. However, HHS employees are not required to speak to the media.

HHS strives to ensure that the media are effectively served within needed deadlines. In order to make certain we provide the media the best possible service and information in a timely fashion, it is important that the relevant agency public affairs office be notified of all media calls/ contacts that employees receive about their HHS work.

Reporters should be informed that the agency's public affairs office coordinates media requests to ensure they receive requested information within their deadline The primary objective for routing reporter calls to the agency public affairs office is to ensure an effective, timely and coordinated agency and departmental response.

Additionally, depending on the context for the interview and the subject matter, the caller may be referred to another HHS agency that has primary expertise in that area. In some instances, the caller may need to be referred to another federal department or agency, if the matter lies within its jurisdiction. Finally, in certain circumstances, the department must decline to comment. These instances include, but are not limited to, pending legal matters; pending requests from Congress, states, or other organizations; procurement-sensitive information; and issues not under HHS jurisdiction.

HHS will release information consistent with the department's Open Government principles and with the Freedom of Information Act (FOIA) provisions. This policy does not override disclosure exemptions under the FOIA. Examples of information not releasable under this policy include, without limitation, information that is, or is marked as, classified information, procurement-sensitive information, information subject to the Privacy Act, information that would violate patient confidentiality, and other controlled unclassified information.

Unless approved by ASPA, communications that include promotion of HHS-funded activities and events will not be conducted by non-HHS outside entities such as public relations agencies. Such activities and events will be reviewed by ASPA on a case-by-case basis.

Procedures Regarding Provision of Information to the News Media

General. Major news media-related activities and efforts shall be coordinated with involved agencies, offices, or programs including review by the appropriate policy, subject matter and technical experts to ensure scientific, technical, and programmatic accuracy.

Coordination of press releases and media material. ASPA will coordinate the review and clearance of departmental press materials by appropriate officials, provide advance notification of the actual release, and be apprised of and seek clearance for, efforts by contractors and outside agencies that are designated to promote coverage for departmental events or topics.

Interviews. In response to media interview requests, an agency public affairs office should identify the most knowledgeable spokesperson(s) who can provide the requested information.

- In general, reporters, including bloggers, should have access to HHS employees they seek to interview. While speaking to the media is not a requirement, employees are encouraged to speak to reporters about their work whenever possible and appropriate.
- When approached by a reporter, HHS employees should work with their immediate supervisor and coordinate with the appropriate public affairs office/personnel in their agency.
- Agency public affairs officers should facilitate interviews and work to meet reporters' deadlines.
- Only HHS employees can speak to the media on behalf of his/her agency. Contractors, fellows (except Title 42 fellows), and other non-federal employees employed by HHS cannot speak on behalf of his/her agency. Exceptions to this practice may be considered on an individual basis.
- Meetings that are open to the public are, by definition, open to the media. HHS employees who are presenters at public events, such as conferences or meetings, are encouraged to accommodate requests from media present regarding their presentation while on site. Interviews or media questions that are beyond the scope of the study or specific work should be referred to their agency public affairs office for appropriate follow up.
- As a matter of routine, media interviews should be on the record and attributable to the person speaking to the media representative, unless an alternate attribution arrangement is mutually agreed upon in advance. HHS recognizes the following types of attribution:
  - **On the record:** All statements are directly quotable and attributable, by name and title, to the person making the statement.

- ○ **On Background:** All statements are directly quotable, but cannot be attributed by name or specific title to the person commenting.
- ○ **On Deep Background:** Anything that is said in the interview is usable but not in direct quotation and not for attribution. The reporter writes it on his or her own.
- ○ **Off the Record:** Information is for the reporter's use only and is not to be printed or made public in any way. The information also is not to be taken to another source in hopes of getting confirmation.

Embargoes. Often HHS issues can be technical, complex and difficult to translate into plain language so extra time can help reporters understand and write about them. The practice of providing embargoed news announcements and background materials, as well as access to subject matter experts, in advance of an announcement can assist the news media in understanding the substance and importance of the announcement, and provide sufficient time to read the information and get necessary clarifications from the agency prior to press time. Given the varied nature of agency missions, agencies may have varied approaches to managing embargoed information. In general, however, HHS agencies may provide embargoed materials when:

- • The issue is not related to regulatory or enforcement issues and does not contain confidential, commercial information, and
- • The information is being published in a journal or other publication that imposes an embargo; or
- • The subject is complex or technical and early access to materials and subject matter experts will help reporters prepare their articles in a timely, accurate manner with the context needed to understand the material.

During an embargo period, reporters may share embargoed material provided by an agency with non-journalists or third parties to obtain quotes or opinions prior to an embargo lift provided that the reporter secures agreement from the third-party to uphold the embargo.

Letters to the Editor and Opinion-Editorial Columns. Letters to the editor and opinion-editorial (op-ed) columns, if designed to represent an official agency response or view, or if the author is writing as part of his/ her official responsibilities, must be cleared through ASPA.

Editorial Boards. Participation by HHS representatives in media-sponsored editorial boards must be cleared and coordinated with ASPA.

Organized Media Events. All departmental-sponsored, organized media events require approval by ASPA. Participation by HHS representatives in organized media events sponsored by other government, private sector, or non-profit organizations must be cleared and coordinated with ASPA.

Journal Articles. Scientific, technical, and policy articles or commentaries written by HHS employees for publication in peer-reviewed journals or other scientific, technical or policy publications are not subject to review by ASPA. However, any press materials that are developed in conjunction with the publication of a journal article fall under the same provision guidelines as outlined above. In addition, agency public affairs offices should notify ASPA of any newsworthy journal articles that are planned for publication regardless of whether press materials are planned.

Procedures Regarding Release of Information to News Media by an Employee in a Personal Capacity

HHS employees who present personal or individual views must make clear that they are presenting their personal and/or individual views—not the views of HHS—and they should not be sourced as an HHS representative or make reference to their official title or position in the piece. This provision includes authorship of letters to the editors and opinion-editorial columns. In addition, such letters to the editors or opinion-editorial columns should not be provided on HHS letterhead.

Procedures Regarding the Use of Social Media

Social media includes online engagement platforms such as Facebook, Twitter, and YouTube. HHS agencies are encouraged to use these channels as ways of disseminating information to the news media. For general guidelines on social media, HHS employees should consult https://www.hhs.gov/web/social-media/index.html.

Appendix B

City of Sault Ste. Marie Media Policy

	The City of Sault Ste. Marie	C-I-15
	Information Manual	

Subject: Media Relations
Service Area: Corporate Services
Division: Corporate Communications
Approved: September 11, 2017
Supersedes: August, 2005

Purpose:
A strategic approach to media relations is required to build an equally beneficial and trusting relationship with news media in order to foster accurate and fair reporting; increase positive news coverage; and protect and enhance the City's reputation and integrity. This policy provides general principles and guidelines to facilitate the release of information and interaction with the media regarding the City of Sault Ste. Marie's policies, programs and services.

This document outlines who can interact with the media in an official capacity on behalf of the City and when, how, and why to initiate or respond to inquiries from print, broadcast, online and social media outlets.

Corporate Communications leads the organization's media relations activities; however, all City departments have a role to play in building professional and cooperative relationships and to ensure media inquiries are responded to in a timely manner that is accurate and clear, and by the most appropriate City spokesperson.

Scope:
Media relations are managed by Corporate Communications on behalf of the organization. This policy applies to all City employees including

The City of Sault Ste. Marie   C-I-15
Information Manual

full-time and part-time workers, casual and temporary staff, as well as
students, volunteers and interns. It addresses how employees interact with
traditional (i.e. print, radio, TV), online and social media sources.

Definitions:

Media includes traditional news sources (print, radio, and television),
online (websites) and social media (blogs, Facebook, LinkedIn, YouTube,
Twitter) and other sites where content is generated by users.

City spokesperson is an employee who has the authority to make statements to traditional, online and social media outlets on behalf of the
organization. Unless otherwise authorized, the City's spokespersons are:

1. **Mayor or acting Mayor (in the mayor's absence):** The Mayor or
   acting Mayor, in cases of the Mayor's absence, shall be the chief
   spokesperson at all times for the City of Sault Ste. Marie representing City Council.
2. **City Councillors:** City Councillors shall be spokespersons on
   events or issues of personal interest to them. It is understood that
   comments and communications from a councillor represent the
   views of the councillor and not necessarily the formal position of
   the City of Sault Ste. Marie.
3. **Chief Administrative Officer:** The Chief Administrative Officer
   shall be the chief staff spokesperson and speaks on behalf of the
   municipality regarding all functions of the organization.
4. **Executive and Senior Management Team members (EMT,
   SMT):** The EMT and SMT of City department shall speak on behalf of his / her area of accountability and responsibility as the chief
   spokesperson for the department.
5. **Signatories of a specific report:** Authors and signatories on a report that is brought before City Council shall provide clarification
   or background to the media on a specific report's content prior to
   its consideration by Council. However, staff shall not give their
   opinion on such reports (including recommendations) before

The City of Sault Ste. Marie   C-I-15
Information Manual

Council makes a decision on the report or comment on decisions
of Council.

6. **Corporate Communications Officer**: The Corporate Communications Officer is the official City spokesperson overseeing communication strategy and media relations for the Corporation.

7. **Other employees as directed or delegated by EMT or SMT**: Staff may provide background information to the media that is publicly available only when directed to do so by EMT or SMT. Requests for interviews shall be referred to the appropriate spokesperson or department head. Staff members can be delegated / designated the duties of spokesperson on issues concerning programs, operations and activities that fall within their area of responsibility, where authorized by the Chief Administrative Officer or department head.

Police, Fire and Emergency Medical Service employees follow their own media guidelines and protocol that govern their procedures. Corporate Communications should nevertheless be made aware of individuals speaking to the media on behalf of the Corporation.

Communications Guiding Standards of Practice

The Corporation's media relations are conducted in conformance with the following principles:

- Work collaboratively to respond to all media queries in a timely way. This may include media contacts outside traditional office hours or days of work.
- Make available the most appropriate spokesperson(s) based on accountability and responsibility and consider the wide range of communication tools available to address the needs associated with each unique circumstance.
- The Corporation reserves the right to time news releases and events in ways that are most beneficial to its own interests. This recognizes that media have different timing requirements.

The City of Sault Ste. Marie   C-I-15
Information Manual

- Communications prepared by the Corporation conform to professional journalistic practices and standards in terms of style,
  content and timing and will support two-way symmetrical communication engagement opportunities with the media.
- The Corporation recognizes that Council and staff should have
  the opportunity to learn about major developments from the
  Corporation first. Accordingly, efforts will be taken to post news
  releases and messages appropriately.

Media Contacts

The Corporate Communications Officer or City Clerk is the designated
management contact for media activity whether initiated by the City or
by media outlets. The centralization of this role ensures consistency and
responsiveness.

Any employee who receives media calls or requests for information should
refer them to the Corporate Communications Officer or City Clerk for
processing.

The Communications Officer, City Clerk or designate is the official
spokesperson for the City. This role involves both direct media responses
and the coordination of media responses in which the CAO, Executive
Management and / or Senior Management employees are interviewed or
featured. Such involvement is dependent on a variety of factors including
the sensitivity of the news item, news value of the item and the availability /
sustainability of official spokespersons for interview.

The Corporate Communications Officer or City Clerk must determine
when responses are appropriate from others in the organization and facilitate such responses.

Members of the organization are encouraged to identify achievements or
activities that may be newsworthy. When they identify such items, they
should contact Corporate Communications for guidance and assistance.

The City of Sault Ste. Marie   C-I-15
Information Manual

As appropriate, subject matter experts will be interviewed by the media. These interviews provide opportunities to promote awareness of staff, projects and programs as well as provide recognition for members of the organization. The Corporate Communications Officer may provide guidance and assistance to those who are the subject of media interviews.

The Spokesperson Role

A spokesperson may share or delegate their responsibility when the subject matter expertise / information is sought beyond what the spokesperson could provide, and when the delegated spokesperson is not adequately prepared to undertake this responsibility.

Following media interviews, City spokespeople are required to email Corporate Communications and any other relevant staff providing the following information:

- the media outlet and reporter
- the interview topic and a brief summary of questions and responses
- date and time when the article, online post or broadcast is expected to be published or aired

Representing the Corporation as a spokesperson:
Any communications that employees make in a professional capacity must not:

I. Breach confidentiality, for example:
   - Reveal confidential intellectual property or information owned by the Corporation or information that is subject of a closed City Council meeting pursuant to the Municipal Act;
   - Release confidential information about an individual (such as a colleague or partner) or organization (such as a stakeholder or partnership agreement) or;

The City of Sault Ste. Marie   C-I-15
Information Manual

- Discuss the Corporation's internal workings (such as working agreements or its future business plans that have not been communicated to the public) or;

II. Do anything that could be considered discriminatory against, or bullying, or harassment of any individual, for example by:

- Making offensive comments relating to race, sex, gender, disability, sexual orientation, religion, age or;

III. Bring disgrace on the Corporation, for example by:

- Criticizing or arguing with colleagues, partners or competitors or;
- Posting or sharing images or links that are inappropriate or;

IV. Breach copyright, for example by:

- Using someone else's images or written content without permission or;
- Failing to give acknowledgement where permission has been given to reproduce something.

Non-spokespeople

Employees who **are** not authorized spokespeople must refer all media inquiries to the authorized spokesperson for the department or project and immediately notify Corporate Communications. This excludes access to routine publicly available information in which City employees are permitted to answer to members of the public (e.g. committee meeting dates, building permit information normally available to the public). Nothing in this policy is intended to prevent the access of information to the public that is normally available.

City employees who are not designated spokespeople are not authorized to make statements to the media and / or in public discussion on behalf of the City. City staff who are not designated spokespersons and who are contacted by a news media representative shall:

- Be courteous and professional.
- Explain that they are not a spokesperson for the City and respectfully decline the request for an interview or information.

The City of Sault Ste. Marie   C-I-15
Information Manual

An appropriate response to the media would be: "I do not have the information for you regarding that topic. I will forward your request to the Communications Officer who will respond to you as soon as possible."

- Provide timely responses to the media by collecting the following information to be forwarded to Corporate Communications:
  - Journalist's name and who they work for
  - Contact number of the journalist or news agency
  - Journalist's deadline
  - Topic of the interview

(Refer to Appendix B: Media Tracking form)

Policy application

Subject to applicable collective agreements and employment agreements, the City may consider disciplinary measures or legal action if an identifiable employee makes defamatory or otherwise inappropriate statements in a public domain about their co-workers and / or employer. This includes comments made on websites, blogs and social media networks using personal computers, Smartphones or devices, from an online account or profile associated with a personal email address.

Employees should be aware that the use of media relations in a way that is unfavourable or malicious may lead to disciplinary action under the City's Code of Conduct. Employees that contact the media without first notifying Corporate Communications, and / or who cause serious damage to the Corporation may lead to action up to and including dismissal.

Monitoring

The City of Sault Ste. Marie and its various online websites and social media accounts are monitored by Corporate Communications. Various monitoring sites ensure the Corporation receives information almost instantly once "City of Sault Ste. Marie" is mentioned. Corporate Communications prompts corrective action when required to ensure the Corporation is not at risk.

The City of Sault Ste. Marie   C-I-15
Information Manual

Known or potentially contentious issues

All media inquiries regarding known or potentially contentious issues must be immediately referred to Corporate Communications and the appropriate person on the Executive Management Team (EMT). In collaboration with the EMT member, Corporate Communications will coordinate a plan and / or response on behalf of the City.

Crisis or emergency issues

During an emergency, the procedure for working with the media is outlined in the City's Crisis Communications Procedure and Emergency Plan. Under the Procedure and the Plan, a designated Information Officer is the main point of contact for the media.

Use of Logos and Branding

Unauthorized use of the Corporation of the City of Sault Ste. Marie name, logo or trademarks without the express permission of an authorized official of the Corporation is strictly prohibited. Logos shall not be altered in any way and will be prominently displayed. Only logos and imagery provided by Corporate Communications will be approved. Refer to the City's Corporate Identity Guidelines for details.

Content Strategy—Use of Voice

The popularity of social media and other media platforms has changed the way the Corporation communicates. It's important to speak to stakeholders in a language that is approachable, friendly, easy-to-read and understand and that speaks conversationally in all facets of communication. The voice used in traditional media, web, social media communications and content is warm, welcoming and engaging, using a personal and respectful tone at all times.

Training

Staff training will be offered in a variety of formats:

- Spokespersons will be trained to measure the success or failure of news items

The City of Sault Ste. Marie   C-I-15
Information Manual

- Social media information sessions will be included in new employee and student orientation sessions
- Upon request, Corporate Communications may provide assistance

Policy Updates

The City of Sault Ste. Marie's Corporate Communication will monitor and update this policy as required.

News Release or Advisory

- The initiative for the development of all news media communication is the responsibility of the individual department and the department's spokesperson.
- The Corporate Communications Officer will be a resource when preparing the spokesperson in the preparation of news releases and in the organization of news conferences.
- Corporate Communications must be notified two-weeks in advance or as soon as possible prior to an event or activity in order to ensure ample time to format information for various media platforms and to provide advance notice to media outlets for scheduling purposes.
- Corporate Communications should be involved in promoting outreach initiatives to the community. This includes open houses, information sessions and future plans where constituents are involved and affected.
- Whenever a member of staff initiates a news release, regardless of the purpose, a copy of the news release must be sent to the Corporate Communications Officer, or their designate **before** it is released to the media or public. The Corporate Communications Officer, or their designate, will review the news release and, if approved, they will distribute it to all appropriate media.

The City of Sault Ste. Marie   C-I-15
Information Manual

- When initiating a release on behalf of the City and quoting any City staff or elected official, the release must be approved in writing by the person being quoted in advance of its release.
- The release must include a contact phone number and email of the corporate spokesperson as the source of the news release (Appendix A). All staff and officials identified as a contact should be available for comment during the day in which the release is issued.
- Corporate Communications reserves the right to determine which media relations tool is most appropriate to use in certain circumstances (Appendix A).

As soon as possible, the Corporate Communications Officer shall forward news releases, public meetings, notices and advisories to the following officials and staff before sending to the media in the order below:

- Mayor and Members of Council where applicable
- The CAO, Deputy CAOs and or respective SMT member where applicable.
- All City Staff
- Media

News releases are posted to the City's website by the Web Content Coordinator or designate.

Responding to Council's Actions

Staff must not make judgmental comments regarding individual Council members, Council actions or City policy when responding to media enquiries. Staff should also refrain from anticipating an action or position that has not been formally taken by City Council or the City. Any enquiry regarding a specific Council member's decision should be forwarded to the Council member.

The City of Sault Ste. Marie   C-I-15
Information Manual

Council members are accessible to the news media and every attempt should be made to encourage the news media representative to contact Council members directly. Telephone numbers and e-mail addresses for all Council members are available on the City website, as well as in printed form in the Clerk's Department.

Litigation, including prosecutions

Staff should not respond to media enquiries regarding City litigation or legal issues. News media enquiries regarding legal matters should be referred to the city solicitor.

Appendix A: Media Relations Tools

There is a diverse range of techniques and tools that can be utilized to reach audiences through the media to deliver messages that are on target, accurate and effective. Media relations should be handled by Corporate Communications or a specialist with experience in working with the media. It is up to the discretion of Corporate Communications to determine which Media Relations tool is most appropriate to use in each circumstance.

The techniques of media relations are part of a larger strategy that Corporate Communications develops on an annual basis. While Corporate Communications need to have the capacity to react quickly to events, most techniques can be prepared in advance and planned carefully.

In addition to staying informed about activities of the City of Sault Ste. Marie departments, Corporate Communications will benefit from closely watching political and social happenings in the community and in the country that are of relevance to, or might influence the organization.

This will ensure that spokespersons are not caught off guard when the media brings issues to their attention and requests a comment (whether or not the questions warrant comment). Staying informed will allow

The City of Sault Ste. Marie   C-I-15
Information Manual

Corporate Communications to predict questions or concerns which might arise and create responses to potential questions.

News Releases
News Releases are issued when there is something newsworthy to announce such as a major service change or a new City initiative. The message must be written for journalists and must be part of the overall Corporate Communications Plan. As a guideline, staff may consider:

- That the news being released is "newsworthy"
- A news release as an introduction to a subject, inviting the news media and others to make further enquiries or to seek an interview on a particular subject matter
- That news releases should be limited to one page
- Avoiding technical or complicated jargon. As a general rule, keep paragraphs to two to three sentences in length.
- Using direct quotes from a spokesperson to make the release more effective and relevant.
- Spelling out numbers one through nine (except for dates, times, age or money). For all other numbers, use numerals (e.g., 10, 11, 12 etc.)
- Proofreading, spell checking and date and time verification
- Being mindful of news media deadlines
- Additional background information may be provided in the form of a media kit that may include fact sheets, background information, multimedia content and contacts

Media Advisory
A media advisory invites the media to an event happening at the City at a specific date, time and place to which the media is invited.

Public Service Announcement
A public service announcement is a message in the public interest with the objective of raising awareness of an upcoming event or activity.

The City of Sault Ste. Marie   C-I-15
Information Manual

Media Events / Photo Opportunities

Media Events provide an excellent opportunity for media to see a City initiative, service, program or facility in action. Such events allow the City to communicate directly with authorized spokespeople and the media.

News Conferences

A news conference is a means of conveying more information that can be carried in a single press release. It is also a way of providing a venue for all media to gather and ask questions of the City's authorized spokespeople.

Interviews

One-on-one interviews allow the media to have a more in-depth and focused discussion with a City spokesperson. It is best if interviews are scheduled through Corporate Communications. An interviewee may benefit from reviewing talking points to guide his or her answers prior to participating in the interview and should be experienced in talking with the media. Corporate Communications may suggest certain topics to focus; a skilled interviewee will know how to redirect conversations back to topics of importance.

Website

The City's news section on its website provides a one-stop location for media and the public that is constantly updated by the addition of new material as it becomes available.

Social Media Platforms

The City subscribes to various platforms including but not limited to Facebook, Twitter, YouTube, Instagram, LinkedIn.

City of Sault Ste. Marie

News Release
For Immediate Release

Create Interest with an Attention Grabbing Headline

Sault Ste. Marie, ON (Year Month Date)—The first paragraph contains the most important information. The reader should be able to tell what the release is about from the first paragraph.

All information in your news release should be written in plain, easily understandable language. The second paragraph can identify the timing, location or significance of the release.

Add a quote from the subject matter expert. Quotes highlight certain aspects of your story and provide another perspective other than that of the writer.

In the remaining space, expand on any details of the matter. Remember your news release should cover who, what, where, when, why as well as how.

All news releases should contain the spokesperson as the contact that the media can follow up with for more details.

-30-
(adding "-30-" identifies the end of the news release)

Media Contact:
Name
Job Title
Service Area
City of Sault Ste. Marie
Phone
Email

Appendix B: Media Tracking Form

City of
Sault Ste. Marie

Media Tracking Form

Date of media call or inquiry: _____

Journalist's name and media outlet: _____

Contact number of the Journalist or news agency: _____

Journalist's deadline: _____

Topic of discussion:

_____

_____

_____

_____

_____

_____

Questions Asked:

_____

_____

_____

_____

_____

Type of interview (on camera, telephone): _____

Staff who responded: _____

Was a News Release issued? Yes No

Air Date / Publication date: _____

Other important information:

_____

_____

_____

_____

_____

Please return to Corporate Communications for tracking purposes.

About the Authors

donalee Moulton

donalee Moulton has written for more than 100 publications globally. She has freelanced for television and radio. donalee is the owner of Quantum Communications and has provided media training and media relations for organizations in the public, private, and nonprofit sectors. She is the author of *The Thong Principle: Saying What You Mean and Meaning What You Say* and *Better Policy/Better Performance: The Who, Why, and What of Organizational Policy*.

Clare O'Connor

Clare O'Connor is a writer, communications specialist, and Certified Change Management Professional (CCMP). She has written for countless media outlets, led corporate communications teams, and delivered training on strategic communications and effective media relations. Clare is the author of *Skateboard Sibby*, a middle-grade novel about change and resilience, and coauthor of *Celebrity Court Cases: Trials of the Rich and Famous*.

Index

www.ingramcontent.com/pod-product-compliance
Lightning Source LLC
Chambersburg PA
CBHW061331220326
41599CB00026B/5138